BALLET BARRE
AND CENTER COMBINATIONS

BALLET BARRE AND CENTER COMBINATIONS

Combinations by

Linda A. Crist

Basil Thompson

Michael Simms

Jeffery Bullock

Margaret McLaughlin Blair

A Dance Horizons Book
Princeton Book Company, Publishers
Hightstown, New Jersey

Labanotation and descriptions checked by Judy Coopersmith, a Labanotator certified by the Dance Notation Bureau.

ISBN 0-87127-220-2

A Dance Horizons Book
Princeton Book Company, Publishers
P.O. Box 831
Hightstown, NJ 08520

Composition by Doric Lay Publishers

CONTENTS

✢

PREFACE: A HISTORY OF
BALLET BARRE AND CENTER COMBINATIONS

My book *Ballet Barre Enchaînements*, originally published in 1994, contained Labanotation and descriptions of barre combinations for various levels of expertise. In order to reach a greater audience, my publisher thought it would be interesting to include this earlier book with a new offering of ballet center combinations. Instead of one large book containing both Labanotation and descriptions of barre and center combinations, three books have been developed. One contains only descriptions of the barre and center combinations; the second provides original music by Dr. Suzanne Knosp, and the third contains the Labanotation of all combinations.

The ballet center section contains combinations taught by guest ballet teachers in residence at the University of Iowa in the spring of 1991: Basil Thompson, Michael Simms, Jeffery Bullock, and Margaret McLaughlin Blair. Their diversity is represented by their affiliations with major companies such as the Royal Ballet, Joffrey Ballet, Royal Winnipeg Ballet, Pacific Northwest Ballet, San Francisco Ballet, and Hamburg Ballet.

Written notes were made of combinations taught both in Majors Ballet I (intermediate level) and Majors Ballet III (advanced level), and formal interviews were taped.

After the guest teachers had departed, a complete documentation of their classes was forwarded for their review and approval.

It should be noted that this is not a compilation of classes, but rather a selection of exercises or one day's classwork that can be utilized when deemed appropriate.

The combinations included in this book can be valuable to the reader in a variety of ways. Teachers who are often unable to attend workshops or study with others may turn to these examples as teaching aids. They give teachers the opportunity to see ballet from different and stimulating perspectives. The steps may be arranged in an unfamiliar order, stress a different concept, or be more challenging rhythmically. I hope you will enjoy the variety it offers.

ACKNOWLEDGMENTS

Many thanks go to the guest teachers without whom this book would not have been possible. I thank them for their patience, graciousness and sense of humor—they updated their bios a number of times and probably thought this project would never reach fruition.

To Helen Chadima who helped make the publication of this book possible.

To my mentor, Françoise Martinet, whose dedication to dance is an inspiration to us all. Since I have been privileged to take her classes for many years, it is only natural that I have assimilated many of the gems that she developed during her teaching tenure. Thank you for being a positive influence in my growth as a teacher. Ms. Martinet was also instrumental in encouraging me to "Americanize" the ballet vocabulary found in these descriptions.

My relationship with Dr. Suzanne Knosp spans many years. She was the departmental accompanist at the University of Iowa before moving on to the University of Arizona. She was at UI in 1991 when the guest teachers were in residence. Originally, this book was going to contain only Labanotation and descriptions of the exercises; then Suzanne expressed an interest in joining me in this endeavor. Her initial intent was to provide typical balletic music to complement the exercises, but she later expressed the desire to compose original music instead. I'm so pleased Suzanne selected the latter option, for her music is magical.

To my husband, Lyndon, who once again contributed graphics and had the patience to edit the numerous pages.

Last but not least, kudos to the dancers: Jason Alt, Marilyn Bordwell, Sally Donaubauer, Laura Gates, Tammy Goetsch, Mica Pfiffner, Holly Stephens, Arianne Stevens, and Amanda Wallace. They spent two very hot and humid weeks in July learning all the combinations so that a video could be made. This allowed me to check the accuracy of my notation and offered Suzanne the opportunity to reexamine her musical selections and determine tempi.

DESCRIPTION GLOSSARY

Counting

$^2/4$ and $^4/4$ meter
   Described by count, i.e., one measure of $^2/4$ = 2 cts.

$^3/4$ meter (Waltz)
   Described in "dancer's counts," i.e., one measure = 1 ct.

$^3/4$ meter (Mazurka, Polonaise)
   Described by count because of the slower tempo, i.e., one measure = 3 cts.

$^6/8$ meter
   Described in dancer's counts, i.e., one measure = 2 cts.

As the last two-meter signatures occur with less frequency, the descriptive material will remind the reader in advance how the enchaînement meter has been counted.

Dancer's counts of introductions: When teachers give a preparation to begin a combination, they often say *and* (&) or *and a* (&a). For example, the *and* in $^6/8$ refers to the second pulse (cts. 4–6) in the measure, and in $^3/4$ *and u* is actually referring to cts. 2–3 of the introduction measure. As dancers and accompanists do not find this problematic, it is used in the descriptions.

The Music: a companion book, *Ballet Barre and Center Combinations: Music*, is available through Princeton Book Company, Publishers, and contains music, scored for piano, specifically designed to accompany these exercises.

Arm Movement

Ballet Barre Combinations

1. A majority of the combinations, except for a few that begin facing, or with the back to, the barre, begin with the left side of the body to the barre and the left

arm placed on the barre. It was therefore not necessary to include the left arm's movement inside parentheses. As is indicated before each barre section, arm movement in the parentheses is only for the right arm, but exceptions will be noted. Exceptions will occur when the dancer turns to face the other side or when the arm movement might be unclear.

2. Abbreviations of the Cecchetti arm positions are as follows:
   Fifth en bas = L5
   Fifth en avant = M5
   Fifth en haut = H5
   Second = 2nd

Ballet Center Combinations

1. All arm movements are included within parentheses. The slash mark separates left arm movement from right. The hyphen separates movement the arms make in transition from one position to the next.

2. Arm movement examples:
   a. (M5-2nd-L5): This indicates simultaneous movement for both arms. They begin fifth en avant, then move to second and finish fifth en bas.
   b. (H5/2nd): The indication to the left of the slash (H5) refers to the left arm and vice versa. The left arm is fifth en haut and the right arm is in second position.
   c. (M5-H5/2nd): Both arms begin in fifth en avant, then move to Cecchetti fourth position en haut—the left arm ends fifth en haut and the right arm ends in second.
   d. (H5/2nd-M5-2nd/H5-rt. 2nd): Arms begin in Cecchetti fourth position en haut with the left arm fifth en haut and the right arm in second—both arms move to fifth en avant—both arms move to fourth position en haut, with the left arm in second and the right arm fifth en haut. Only the right arm moves to second, thereby ending with both arms in second position.

3. Grand port de bras: Since no description of the arm movement is given, it is assumed that a circular port de bras would be performed, i.e., the arms move toward the upstage and finish downstage.

4. Windmill arm variations:
   a. The change from one arabesque to another is a "swimming backstroke" motion: In first arabesque, the forward arm moves upward and back while the back arm moves downward and forward to arrive in second arabesque. (Basil Thompson's Grand Adagio #6, meas. 1–3.)
   b. The change from Cecchetti fourth en haut to the reverse arm position: Begin H5/2nd and in the transition the left arm moves slowly to 2nd as the right

arm moves swiftly down to L5 through M5 to H5. Arms should arrive simultaneously. (Jeffery Bullock's Grand Adagio #2, meas. 15–16, and Margaret McLaughlin Blair's Grand Adagio #2, meas. 28–29.)

5. H5 in relation to the spine: The arm direction relates to the verticality of the spine—up is toward the head and down is toward the tail bone. When vertical, an H5 arm can be described as being "headward"—above the top of the spine or above its point of attachment, the shoulder. This relationship is maintained even when the torso is tilted forward in a port de bras. The arm is considered H5 because it has maintained its relationship to the spine.

Arabesque

1. Croisé first arabesque: This arabesque has a croisé relationship to the audience rather than an effacé relationship. Face DSR with the left leg as a support and the right leg raised croisé derrière. The arm on the side of the support [the left] is forward, whereas the right arm is taken to the side a little behind the second position. There is no rotation/twist of the torso or shoulders.

2. Russian fourth arabesque: The arms and legs are in the same relationship as croisé first arabesque but there is an inclusion—a twist/spiral—which occurs in the torso. Turn the torso away from the audience and try to show your back to the audience. The head is turned toward the audience.

3. Croisé second arabesque: The legs are in the same relationship to the audience as in croisé first arabesque. The arms are reversed, with the right arm forward in opposition to the support, and the left extended to the side a little behind second position. The head looks forward toward the right arm.

Leg Movement (Gesture)

1. Abbreviations for supports and gestures are as follows:
   R = right support or gesture
   L = left support or gesture

2. Three retiré positions used in the descriptions and Labanotation are as follows:
   a. Retiré front (devant): Toe touches in front under the knee.
   b. Retiré side (passé): Toe touches at the side of the knee.
   c. Retiré back (derrière): Toe touches behind the knee.

3. Three cou-de-pied positions used in the descriptions and Labanotation are as follows:

a. Cou-de-pied front (devant): Little toe touches just above the ankle bone and the foot is fully pointed. If a wrapped position front is desired, it will be indicated.

b. Cou-de-pied side: Toe touches the achilles tendon and the foot is fully pointed.

c. Cou-de-pied back (derrière): Heel is placed behind the supporting foot and the foot is fully pointed.

4. Balançoire or en cloche: A transitional movement in which the action of brushing the leg backward or forward through first position ends with the gesture leg raised at right angles to the hip. There is no tipping of the body, nor is the action done forcefully.

5. Demi-hauteur: Leg at approximately 45-degree angle; slightly above dégagé height.

6. Hauteur: Leg raised at right angle to the hip.

7. Rotation: The opposite of a fouetté. When the leg is extended back, the pivot is inward or toward the gesture leg, finishing with that leg side or front depending on the amount of pivot.

Definition of Steps

Reference Materials: *Technical Manual and Dictionary of Classical Ballet*, 3rd ed. by Gail Grant (Dover Publications, NY, 1982); *The Bournonville School*, edited by Kirsten Ralov, with Labanotation by Ann Hutchinson Guest (Marcel Dekker, NY, 1979); and *Classical Ballet Technique* by Gretchen Ward Warren (University of Florida Presses, Gainesville, 1989).

Ballonné composé de côté: A compound step consisting of a ballonné simple, chassé movement and fermé (closing) to the fifth position.

Bournonville pas de bourrée couru: A running step in fifth position that travels sideways. It skims fleetingly across the stage with slightly bent legs, giving it an earthy feeling, yet it is light and lifted.

Brisé volé: Begin on L with R in low back attitude with toe touching. Step backward on R, brush L through first position to battement back in effacé and immediately brush R back and beat underneath. Land in plié on L with R cou-de-pied back. Step, brisé volé, travels backward.

Cecchetti assemblé coupé: An assemblé started from one foot. The working leg may be cou-de-pied or extended à terre or en l'air. Demi-plié and spring off the support, with the working leg closing in fifth position without a brush.

Fouetté rond de jambe en tournant en dehors: Whipped circle of the leg while turning. Plié on the L leg, at the same time opening R leg to second position en l'air. Relevé on the L, executing a tour en dehors, and whip the R foot in back of, then quickly in front of, the L knee. Plié on L while opening R leg to second position en l'air.

Glissade sur les demi-pointes en tournant en dedans: Begin on L with R tendu front. Demi-rond de jambe en dehors and piqué onto R. Quickly bring L leg front into sous-sus and turn $^3/_4$ rt.; plié on L while continuing the turn $^1/_4$ rt. as R leg disengages front at dégagé height.

Mazurka: Step forward on L in plié and hop, traveling forward with R cou-de-pied side ct.1&; brush R front ct.2; hop again on L and travel forward ct.&3. The center of gravity does not change on the hops, thereby causing the movement to remain close to the floor, producing a "scooting" or "chugging" action.

Pas de basque sauté en avant: This is done in the same manner as the pas de basque glissé but jumped. The demi-rond de jambe en dehors is done à la demi-hauteur; after the spring to the side onto the R foot, the L foot is brought in just under the R knee. Step forward onto the L and close R in fifth position.

Piqué emboîté en tournant: Begin with L in plié and R dégagé-height front. Demi-rond de jambe en dedans and piqué onto R, making $^1/_2$ tour to the rt. with L retiré front; step L [remain on relevé] in front of R and make $^1/_2$ tour to the rt. with R retiré front.

Posé: Step directly to the demi-point and lower on a straight leg while maintaining the desired position.

Renversé en dehors with relevé: Begin facing DSL in plié with L cou-de-pied back. Step L behind R and throw R to croisé devant en l'air. Execute a grand rond de jambe en l'air en dehors with relevé on L while pivoting $^1/_4$ rt., finishing DSR in attitude back croisé. The R begins pas de bourrée dessous en tournant, during which the body is forcefully bent from the waist to the left and then to the back. The first two movements of the step are done slowly with the pose in attitude held a moment, then with a quick backbend in pas de bourrée.

Sautillée: Arabesques sautillées are hops in arabesque. The center of gravity does not change on the hops, thereby causing the movement to remain close to the floor, producing a "chugging" or "scooting" action.

Sissonne changée en avant: Begin in fifth position demi-plié with R foot back. Spring upward and forward into the air and land in demi-plié on the R with L attitude back. This example does not close in fifth position upon landing.

Sissonne passée front (devant): Begin in fifth position demi-plié with R foot back. Spring upward into the air and land in demi-plié on the L with R cou-de-pied front.

Sissonne passée back (derrière): Begin in fifth position demi-plié with R foot front. Spring upward into the air and land in demi-plié on the L with R cou-de-pied back.

Sissonne simple back (derrière): Begin in fifth position demi-plié with R foot back. Spring upward into the air and land on L with R cou-de-pied back.

Sissonne simple front (devant): Begin in fifth position demi-plié with R foot front. Spring upward into the air and land on L with R cou-de-pied front.

Tour jeté: Grand jeté dessus en tournant.

Frictionless or Non-Swivel Turn

The turning action occurs in the body above the ankle without moving the ball of the foot. Even though the foot has not moved, there is still a change of front; a new facing.

If standing on a turned-out L support and pivoting lt. (en dedans), the resultant position will be a parallel support. If standing on a parallel L support and pivoting rt. (en dehors), the resultant position will be a turned-out L support.

Fourth and Lunge Positions

The fourth and lunge positions may vary in size depending on whether they are used as a preparation or an ending. The descriptive notes indicate three variations:

a. Fourth position demi-plié: An academic position in which both legs are bent in preparation for an outside pirouette.

b. Long fourth position: The position used as a preparation for an inside pirouette or the ending for an outside pirouette. The forward leg is bent and the back leg is straight with the whole foot on the floor.

c. Lunge position: A position most commonly used for grand port de bras and wider than the long fourth position.

Stage Directions

Because a fixed point of reference to the room may vary according to each teacher's personal preference or background, the author has determined that the easiest solution would be to refer to stage areas, as these are a constant and standard form of reference. They are as follows:

DSL = downstage left	DSR = downstage right
SL = stage left	SR = stage right
USL = upstage left	USR = upstage right
DS = downstage	US = upstage

Repeats

In a *repeat to the other side* or *lateral symmetry*, there is an exchange of right and left in the use of the body and in direction for all movements in the enchaînement. A glissade back (derrière) with the right leg back travels to the right side without changing legs. In a *repeat to the other side*, a glissade derrière with the left leg back would travel to the left side with the left leg remaining back.

In *sagittal symmetry* there is an exchange of forward for backward direction [or vice versa] in the enchaînement, but the sideward directions would remain the same. A glissade forward (en avant) with the right leg front will now be performed as a glissade backward (en arrière) with the right leg back, but a glissade traveling to the right would continue to do so with the feet in the same relationship to each other. A jeté over (dessus) would become a jeté under (dessous), etc.

Although a majority of the enchaînements can be *repeated to the other side*, this is not always indicated in the notation or descriptions.

General Comments

Since the descriptions do not include any directions for head movements, it is assumed that the reader would apply the normal balletic head positions and épaulement.

The "Americanization" of ballet terminology: Professor Françoise Martinet strongly recommended the inclusion of our "Americanized" terminology within the descriptive notes. She said, "Why not describe movement as we speak of it in class? Why complicate our lives? Simplify." Since I concur, this suggestion has been implemented. The reader will find *tendu front* rather than *tendu devant* or *jeté over* instead of *jeté dessus*.

General Abbreviations

  arab. = arabesque (arm position)
   ct. = count
   lt. = left (side or direction)
 meas. = measure(s)
   rt. = right (side or direction)

BALLET BARRE COMBINATIONS

Linda A.
Crist

BIOGRAPHY

Linda A. Crist is an associate professor at the University of Iowa where she teaches various levels of ballet and elementary and intermediate Labanotation.

She received her Bachelor's degree in Music and a Master of Arts in Dance from the University of Iowa. After teaching at Ball State University (Muncie, Indiana), Luther College (Decorah, Iowa), she joined the faculty of the University of Iowa in 1977.

Linda began taking Labanotation courses from Judith Allen and continues to pursue her interest in this particular area. She and Judy have reconstructed Charles Weidman's *Brahms Waltzes* and Buzz Miller's *Not for Love Alone.* Her other reconstructions include *Six Fairy Variations* from *The Sleeping Beauty*; Tudor's *Little Improvisations, Aerobic Pas de Deux* and *Les Cygnets*; Bournonville's *Pas de Deux* from *Flower Festival at Genzano*, which was selected for the 1987 ACDFA adjudication; Eglevsky's *Pas de Trois*; Allen's *That All-American Game*; Ming-shen Ku's *Bamboo Grove*; Peter Anastos's *Yes Virginia, Another Piano Ballet*; Doris Humphrey's *Water Study* and, most recently, Valerie Bettis's *The Desperate Heart.*

Linda holds certification in Beginning, Intermediate and Advanced Labanotation; and in 1985 she received her teaching certification from The Ohio State University. For three summers she served as the external evaluator and later codirector with Professor Odette Blum in the teaching of this same certification course. In 1989 and 1990 she was rehearsal director for the 70 children selected to participate in the Joffrey Ballet production of *The Nutcracker.*

Published works include *Ballet Center Work* (1988), a compilation of combinations by Françoise Martinet; *threebythree* (1991) and the Macintosh version of *CLIP (Computerized Labanotation Instructional Program)* (1991). Professional affiliations include Iowa Alliance of Arts Education, Congress on Research in Dance (treasurer), Dance Notation Bureau and International Council of Kinetography Laban.

INTERVIEW WITH LINDA A. CRIST

❧

How often does an individual have the opportunity to conduct her own interview? Due consideration can be given to each response and one can ignore a question or simply make up another. Here is what I have to say about myself.

LC: As a youngster I studied ballet at local studios in Iowa and Oregon, from third through eighth grade, but I did not have the opportunity to dance again until my sophomore year at the University of Iowa.

Q: *Tell me more about your university dance experience.*

LC: There were no ballet classes offered in the 60s at the University and dance was offered in a small program within the Women's Physical Education Department. Only modern dance classes were available. Because of my previous dance experience, I was placed in the advanced modern dance class, and was that an eye-opener! What were these people doing running around without ballet slippers? What were those weird off-balance combinations and strange shapes? The women in the Physical Education Department probably thought we were all a little strange, too. At that time we were not allowed to walk the hallways in our leotards and tights and had to cover ourselves up between classes.

Q: *Who directed the dance program at that time?*

LC: Marcia Thayer was instrumental in developing dance at the University of Iowa. She taught everything—technique, aesthetics, teaching of dance and history. She and her husband, Dr. David Thayer, were instrumental in making dance visible and educating the public. We gave many concerts throughout the year, toured and were very active in the Theatre Department's numerous musicals. Marcia was an inspiring and challenging teacher who instilled in me a true appreciation for modern dance. My first teaching job was, in fact, a modern position at Ball State University in Muncie, Indiana.

Q: *Did you ever consider going to New York to dance professionally?*

LC: I had given that some thought, but I was told by others that at auditions a wire was strung across the stage at a certain height, and if you weren't tall enough you weren't considered. As I am barely over five feet tall, I decided to forgo this marvelous experience. As a graduate assistant in dance at UI, I found that I really enjoyed teaching, and performance opportunities were plentiful. University teaching beckoned.

Q: *Were you trained in any one specific method?*

LC: My training has been eclectic. I have taken time during the summers to attend Vaganova and Cecchetti Teachers Workshops, which were very enlightening and stimulating.

Q: *What other teachers made an impression on you?*

LC: There have been many others throughout the years, but the person who most influenced me was my mentor, Françoise Martinet, who, prior to her tenure as a dance faculty member at UI from 1978 to 1997, was a principal dancer with the Joffrey Ballet. I was able to take class with the "kids" all of those years. I may have the dubious honor of having studied with her the longest and of being her oldest student! We heard many stories of the Joffrey Ballet and were privy to the teaching innovations of Mr. Joffrey. Her classes were eclectic, demanding, dancey, and she seemed to know how to cajole even the most timid and get results. She is a loved and respected teacher whom the university was truly fortunate to have on faculty.

Q: *Has this influenced your teaching?*

LC: Most assuredly. There were so many instruction "gems" that she imparted to us. The progressions and nit-picking of the basics really worked, and I use them.

Q: *Do you feel you stress one thing beyond all others in your teaching?*

LC: I teach primarily the intermediate-level ballet classes here at UI, plus Labanotation. Many of the students who enroll have had poor instruction—I spend a lot of time working on basics and broadening their technical background. It is heart-wrenching for a student who has taken dance for twelve years to go back to the basics. Our standards are very high here and appropriately so, for the dance world is highly competitive.

Q: *When did Labanotation enter into your life?*

LC: In the late 70s I only taught technique—ballet and modern. If one wanted to remain in academia and be an asset to the department, it was important to develop another area of expertise. When I attended the American College Dance Festival at Connecticut College, I took the Beginning Labanotation course from Odette Blum and thoroughly enjoyed it. At Iowa, Judy Allen taught all the notation courses and I decided to take class with her students. Soon after taking both the elementary and intermediate classes I began teaching them. I had found my special space. Since then I have taken Advanced Labanotation and have received my Teaching Certification from The Ohio State University, where I now codirect this same certification course with Odette Blum.

Q: *Do you have any other thoughts about a career in dance?*

LC: Students are often terribly discouraged when they cannot dance professionally, but there will always be special niches that will enable them to continue doing what they love most. I still take class and am determined to do so as long as I can. It's great for the brain and the body. In summation, just find that special place to dance and do so. Enjoy!

PLIÉ DESCRIPTIONS

⚘

Arm movement indicated in parentheses is only for the right arm. Exceptions will be noted.

Plié #1:

Intermediate level

Music: Adagio #1

First position (rt. 2nd):

meas. 1–2: Demi-plié and straighten in first position (L5-M5).

meas. 3–4: Repeat demi-plié and straighten in first position (L5-2nd).

meas. 5–8: Grand plié and straighten in first position (L5-M5-H5).

meas. 9–12: Press to rise in first position, demi-plié while on relevé, heels to the floor [demi-plié position], straighten supports.

meas. 13–14: Battement tendu R side (2nd) and lower into second position.

meas. 15–16: Demi-plié and straighten in second position (M5-2nd).

meas. 17–32: Repeat meas. 1–16 in second position but close R front in fifth position for the final demi-plié and straighten.

meas. 33–48: Repeat meas. 1–16 in fifth position but close R in first position for the final demi-plié and straighten.

meas. 49–52: Battement tendu R side on fondu, and port de bras toward barre (reach to side-H5 in relation to spine).

meas. 53–54: Stay on fondu and demi-rond de jambe R en dehors to point tendu back as torso folds forward (low M5).

meas. 55–56: Straighten L support as torso unfolds [rolls up sequentially] to vertical (2nd), chest folding forward slightly (L5) on ct. 3 of meas. 56.

meas. 57–62: Cambré back (M5-H5) and return torso to vertical (2nd).

9

meas. 63–64: Close R in first position (L5).

meas. 65–68: Battement tendu R side on fondu and port de bras toward barre (2nd-H5 in relation to spine).

meas. 69–70: Stay on fondu and demi-rond de jambe en dedans R to point tendu front as torso folds forward (low M5).

meas. 71–72: Straighten support as torso unfolds [rolls up sequentially] to vertical (2nd).

meas. 73–80: Fondu with port de bras forward (H5 in relation to spine), straighten L support and return torso to vertical, close R leg in first position (2nd).

Plié #2:

Intermediate level

Music: Adagio #2

In this example, two counts are the equivalent of one measure of 6/8.

First position (rt. 2nd):

meas. 1: Cts. 1–2: Small demi-plié [first degree contraction] in first position and straighten.

meas. 2: Cts. 3–4: Repeat demi-plié [first degree contraction] and straighten.

meas. 3–4: Cts. 5–8: Normal demi-plié [third degree contraction] in first position and straighten.

meas. 5–8: Cts. 1–8: Grand plié in first position (first port de bras), battement tendu R side and lower into second position on ct. 8 of meas. 8.

meas. 9–16: Cts. 1–16: Repeat meas. 1–8 in second position but change to croisé fourth position with R front on ct. 16 of meas. 16.

meas. 17–24: Cts. 1–16: Repeat meas. 1–8 in croisé fourth position but change to fifth position with R front on ct. 16 of meas. 24.

meas. 25–32: Cts. 1–16: Repeat meas. 1–8 in fifth position but remain in fifth position after rising from grand plié.

meas. 33–34: Cts. 1–4: Port de bras forward (H5 in relation to spine).

meas. 35–36: Cts. 5–8: Unroll [sequential movement] through back when returning torso to vertical (keep L5).

meas. 37: Cts. 1–2: Rise to sous-sus (2nd-H5).

meas. 38:   Cts. 3–4: Remain in sous-sus and cambré back.

meas. 39:   Cts. 5–6: Return torso to vertical (2nd).

meas. 40:   Cts. 7–8: Remain in sous-sus (both L5) and balance.

Plié #3:

Advanced level

Music: Adagio #3

First position (rt. 2nd):

meas. 1–2:   Stand in first position (both L5).

meas. 3–4:   Demi-plié in first position (both M5) and straighten in first position (lt. to 2nd and regrasps barre/rt. H5).

meas. 5–6:   Demi-plié in first position (M5-L5) and straighten L with R battement tendu front (2nd).

meas. 7:   Close R in first position, small demi-plié in first position on ct. 3 of meas. 7.

meas. 8:   Straighten supports in first position.

meas. 9–12:   Grand plié in first position (first port de bras) and straighten.

meas. 13–14:   Tilt torso forward until parallel to floor with focus on palm of rt. hand.

meas. 15:   Return torso to vertical.

meas. 16:   Battement tendu R side and lower into second position.

meas. 17–20:   Grand plié in second position (first port de bras).

meas. 21–24:   Repeat grand plié in second position (H5-M5-2nd), (M5) on ct. 3 of meas. 24.

meas. 25–31:   Grand port de bras en dehors.

meas. 32:   Shift lt. and point tendu R side, close front in fifth position.

meas. 33–44:   In fifth position repeat same demi- and grands pliés as described in meas. 1–12.

meas. 45–47:   Cambré back (arm rotates with palm facing ceiling) and return torso to vertical (arm returns to normal rotation).

meas. 48:   Demi-plié in fifth position (L5) and sous-sus.

Plié #4:

Advanced level

Music: Adagio #4

First position (rt. 2nd):

meas. 1:	Demi-plié in first position (L5).
meas. 2:	Battement tendu R front as L support straightens (M5).
meas. 3:	Close R in first position demi-plié.
meas. 4:	Battement tendu L back as R support straightens (arab.).
meas. 5:	Close L in first position demi-plié (M5).
meas. 6:	Relevé in first position (H5).
meas. 7:	Lower with straight supports to first position, press to rise on ct. 3.
meas. 8:	Lower to straight supports in first position.
meas. 9–12:	Grand plié in first position and straighten (M5-L5-2nd).
meas. 13–16:	Port de bras forward and up (H5 in relation to spine), then battement tendu R side and lower into second position.
meas. 17–20:	Grand plié in second position and straighten (M5-L5-2nd).
meas. 21:	Demi-plié in second position on cts. 1–2 of meas. 21, straighten from plié on ct. 3 of meas. 21 (slowly lowers to L5 during meas. 21–22).
meas. 22:	Demi-plié in second position.
meas. 23–24:	Straighten in second position (M5-2nd).
meas. 25–26:	Port de bras toward barre (reach side-H5 in relation to spine).
meas. 27:	Keep torso folded to the lt. as legs change to lunge position in second position with R bending.
meas. 28:	Straighten R in second position [torso still folded].
meas. 29–30:	Grand plié in second position as torso folds front (M5-L5).
meas. 31–32:	Straighten from plié as torso unfolds to vertical (2nd), shift lt. and point tendu R side, close front in fifth position on ct. 3 of meas. 32.
meas. 33:	Demi-plié in fifth position (L5).
meas. 34:	Battement tendu R front as L support straightens (M5).

meas. 35:   Close R front in fifth position demi-plié.

meas. 36:   Battement tendu L back as R support straightens (arab.).

meas. 37:   Close L back in fifth position demi-plié (M5).

meas. 38:   Press to rise [no sous-sus] (H5).

meas. 39:   Lower with straight supports to fifth position on cts. 1–2, press to rise in fifth [no sous-sus] on ct. 3.

meas. 40:   Lower with straight supports to fifth position.

meas. 41–44:   Grand plié in fifth position (M5-L5-2nd) and straighten.

meas. 45–48:   Cambré back (H5 in relation to spine) and return torso to vertical, battement tendu R front (M5-2nd) on cts. 2–3 of meas. 48.

meas. 49–55:   Fondu and grand port de bras en dedans but straighten L support as torso reaches lt. side of the circular movement.

meas. 56:   Temps lié forward, ending with L point tendu back on cts. 1–2, (M5) on ct. 3.

meas. 57–62:   Grand port de bras en dehors but fondu as torso begins circle to front, ending in deep lunge position, toe of L foot touching floor.

meas. 63:   Straighten R support as torso unfolds to vertical (2nd).

meas. 64:   Press to rise, drawing L back into sous-sus, and balance (both H5).

Plié #5:

Beginning level

Music: Adagio #3

First position facing the barre (both arms forward and grasping barre):

meas. 1–2:   Demi-plié in first position and straighten.

meas. 3–4:   Repeat meas. 1–2.

meas. 5–7:   Demi-plié then roll up through feet, ending in relevé.

meas. 8:   Lower to first position with straight supports.

meas. 9–12:   Repeat meas. 5–8.

meas. 13–14:   Battement tendu R side and lower into second position.

meas. 15–16:   Press to rise in second position and lower with straight supports.

meas. 17–28: Repeat meas. 1–12 in second position.

meas. 29–30: Shift lt. and point tendu R side, close front in third position.

meas. 31–32: Press to rise in third position and lower with straight supports.

meas. 33–44: Repeat meas. 1–12 in third position.

meas. 45–46: Battement tendu R side and close in first position.

meas. 47–48: Press to rise in first position and balance (both H5).

Plié #6:

Intermediate level

Music: Adagio #2

In this example, two counts are the equivalent of one measure of 6/8.

First position (rt. 2nd):

meas. 1–2: Cts. 1–4: Demi-plié in first position and straighten (L5-M5).

meas. 3–4: Cts. 5–8: Repeat demi-plié and straighten (2nd-H5).

meas. 5: Cts. 1–2: Press to rise (lt. to H5).

meas. 6: Cts. 3–4: Balance.

meas. 7–8: Cts. 5–8: Demi-plié in first position and straighten (both M5–both 2nd with lt. regrasping barre).

meas. 9–12: Cts. 1–8: Grand plié in first position and straighten (first port de bras).

meas. 13–16: Cts. 1–8: Port de bras forward and up (H5 in relation to spine), battement tendu R side and lower into second position on ct. 8 of meas. 16 (2nd).

meas. 17–28: Cts. 1–24: Repeat meas. 1–12 in second position.

meas. 29–32: Cts. 1–8: Port de bras toward barre (H5 in relation to spine) and return torso to vertical (2nd); shift lt. and point tendu R side, closing front in fifth position on ct. 8 of meas. 32.

meas. 33–44: Cts. 1–24: Repeat meas. 1–12 in fifth position; on the balance press to rise [not a sous-sus], (L5-M5) on ct. 8 of meas. 44.

meas. 45–48: Cts. 1–8: Cambré back (H5 in relation to the spine) and return torso to vertical (2nd-both L5).

Plié #7:

Beginning level

Music: Adagio #5

A very slow 3/4 with dancer's counts arranged in units of six.

First position (both arms forward and grasping barre):

meas. 1: Ct. 1: Demi-plié in first position.

Cts. 2–3: Straighten.

meas. 2: Cts. 4–6: Repeat demi-plié and straighten.

meas. 3: Cts. 1–3: Slow press to relevé.

meas. 4: Ct. 4: Demi-plié in first position.

Cts. 5–6: Straighten supports.

meas. 5–6: Cts. 1–6: Port de bras lt. (release rt. hand from barre-2nd-H5 in relation to spine).

meas. 7: Cts. 1–3: Torso returns to vertical (2nd-M5 regrasping barre).

meas. 8: Cts. 4–6: Battement tendu R side and lower into second position.

meas. 9–12: Cts. 1–12: Repeat meas. 1–4 demi-plié/rise combination in second position.

meas. 13–14: Cts. 1–6: Port de bras rt. (release lt. hand from the barre-2nd-H5 in relation to spine).

meas. 15: Cts. 1–3: Torso returns to vertical (lt. through 2nd to M5, regrasping barre).

meas. 16: Cts. 4–6: Shift lt. and point tendu R side, close front in third position.

meas. 17–20: Cts. 1–12: Repeat meas. 1–4 demi-plié/rise combination in third position.

meas. 21: Cts. 1–3: Rise in third position (H5).

meas. 22: Cts. 4–6: Stay on relevé (lt. H5).

meas. 23: Cts. 1–3: Balance.

meas. 24: Ct. 4: Demi-plié in third position (both M5 and grasping barre).

Cts. 5–6: Straighten R support and battement tendu L side, close front in third position.

meas. 25–32:   Cts. 1–24: Repeat meas. 17–24 in third position with L in front, but in meas. 32 battement tendu R side and close in first position (both L5).

Plié #8:

Advanced level

Music: Adagio #2

In this example, two counts are the equivalent of one measure of 6/8.

Second position (rt. 2nd):

meas. 1–4:   Cts. 1–7: Grand plié in second position and straighten (first port de bras).

Ct. 8: Shift weight lt. with R point tendu side, pivot 1/4 lt. [frictionless pivot] (M5 and grasp barre).

meas. 5:   Cts. 1–2: Resultant position facing barre (parallel lunge position with L bent) is used to stretch back of R leg.

meas. 6:   Cts. 3–4: Retain fondu on L as R draws into a parallel cou-de-pied position in which top of toes slide against floor (metatarsal stretch).

meas. 7:   Cts. 5–6: Remain on fondu and pivot 1/4 rt. [frictionless pivot] while turning out R gesture leg, which still has top of toes against floor (2nd).

meas. 8:   Cts. 7–8: Straighten L as R slides (from top of toes to tip of toes) out to point tendu side and closes in first position.

meas. 9–10:   Cts. 1–4: Demi-plié (L5) and straighten in first position.

meas. 11–12:   Cts. 5–8: Repeat demi-plié and straighten in first position (M5-2nd).

meas. 13–16:   Cts. 1–7: Grand plié and straighten in first position (H5-M5-2nd).

Ct. 8: Battement tendu R side and lower into second position.

meas. 17–24:   Cts. 1–16: Exact repeat of meas. 1–8 in second position but close R front in fifth position.

meas. 25–32:   Cts. 1–16: Exact repeat of meas. 9–16 in fifth position. Remain in fifth position following straightening from grand plié.

meas. 33–36:   Cts. 1–8: Port de bras forward (H5 in relation to spine) and return torso to vertical.

meas. 37–40: Cts. 1–6: Cambré back (M5-L5-rt. back diagonal-H5 in relation to spine) and return torso to vertical.

Cts. 7–8: (M5-2nd).

Plié #9:

First position (rt. 2nd):

meas. 1–2: (Both L5).

meas. 3–4: Demi-plié in first position and straighten (both M5-both H5).

meas. 5–6: Press to rise.

meas. 7–8: Lower with straight legs to first position (both 2nd with lt. regrasping barre).

meas. 9–10: Demi-plié and straighten in first position (M5-2nd).

meas. 11–14: Grand plié and straighten in first position (first port de bras).

meas. 15–16: Battement tendu R side and lower into second position.

meas. 17–30: Repeat meas. 1–14 in second position.

meas. 31–32: Close R front in fifth position.

meas. 33–46: Repeat meas. 1–14 in fifth position (rise in fifth rather than sous-sus).

meas. 47–48: Chassé forward (L5-M5-H5), ending with L point tendu back.

meas. 49: Fold chest forward for a breath and return chest to vertical (M5–L5).

meas. 50–51: Cambré back (back middle-H5 in relation to spine).

meas. 52–54: Return torso to vertical.

meas. 55–56: Chassé L through first to point tendu front (M5-L5-2nd).

meas. 57: (Allongé).

meas. 58–59: Fondu and port de bras forward (H5 in relation to spine).

meas. 60–62: Lengthen torso and return it to vertical with R support straightening; fondu with a release of L to dégagé height in front on ct. 3 of meas. 62.

Intermediate level

Music: Adagio #4

meas. 63: Glissade forward sur les demi-pointes closing R front in sous-sus.

meas. 64: Balance (lt. to H5).

Plié #10:

Intermediate Level

Music: Adagio #6

In this example, two counts are the equivalent of one measure of 6/8.

First position (rt. L5):

meas. 1: Cts. 1–2: Press to rise in first position (M5) and hold.

meas. 2: Ct. 3: Demi-plié in first position.

Ct. 4: Straighten in first position (2nd).

meas. 3: Cts. 5&6: Demi-plié and pulse [down, up, down] (L5).

meas. 4: Cts. 7–8: Straighten supports (M5-2nd).

meas. 5–8: Cts. 1–8: Grand plié and straighten in first position (first port de bras).

meas. 9–11: Cts. 1–6: Port de bras forward (H5 in relation to spine) and return torso to vertical by rolling [sequentially] through spine (space hold on arm results in L5), (M5) on ct. 6 of meas. 11.

meas. 12: Cts. 7–8: Battement tendu R side and lower into 2nd position (2nd-L5).

meas. 13–20: Cts. 1–16: Repeat meas. 1–8 in second position.

meas. 21–22: Cts. 1–4: Port de bras to rt., away from barre (lt. H5 in relation to spine/rt. L5 in relation to spine).

meas. 23: Cts. 5–6: Return torso to vertical (both M5).

meas. 24: Ct. 7: Shift lt. with R point tendu side (both 2nd with lt. regrasping barre).

Ct. 8: Close R front in fifth position (L5).

meas. 25–32: Cts. 1–16: Repeat meas. 1–8 in fifth position.

meas. 33–36: Cts. 1–6: Cambré back (L5-M5-H5) and return torso to vertical (2nd).

Ct. 7: (Allongé).

Ct. 8: (Both L5).

BATTEMENT TENDU DESCRIPTIONS

❧

Arm movement indicated in parentheses is only for the right arm. Exceptions will be noted.

Battement Tendu #1:

> Intermediate level
>
> Music: A Sultry Tune

Fifth position R front (rt. L5):

meas. 1:   Cts. 1–2: Battement tendu R front and close in fifth position.

meas. 2:   Ct. 3: Battement tendu R side.

       Ct. 4: Pas de cheval (slide R leg through fifth front) and flick to cou-de-pied side.

meas. 3:   Ct. 5: Press to fifth position demi-plié with R back.

       Ct. &6: Remain on fondu with R cou-de-pied side, close R front rolling through foot, ending with both supports straight.

meas. 4:   Cts. 7–8: Battement tendu L over.

meas. 5–8:   Cts. 1–8: Sagittal repeat of meas. 1–4 beginning with R battement tendu back and ending with L battement tendu under (M5) on ct. 8 of meas. 8.

meas. 9:   Cts. 1–2: Battement soutenu front (H5).

meas. 10:   Cts. 3–4: Battement soutenu back (arab.-M5 on closing).

meas. 11:   Cts. 5–6: Battement soutenu R under (2nd-L5 on closing).

meas. 12:   Cts. 7–8: Demi-plié and straighten (M5).

meas. 13–16:   Cts. 1–8: Sagittal reverse of meas. 9–12. Arm movement remains the same, i.e., R battement soutenu back (H5), L battement soutenu front (arab.), R battement soutenu over, demi-plié and straighten.

Battement Tendu #2:

Intermediate level

Music: A Sultry Tune

Fifth position R front (rt. M5):

meas. 1:   Cts. 1–2: Battement tendu R front, flex toes.

meas. 2:   Cts. 3–4: Flex ankle, "point" ankle.

meas. 3:   Cts. 5–6: "Point" toes, close R in fifth position.

meas. 4:   Cts. 7–8: Demi-plié in fifth position, then straighten L support and battement tendu R side (2nd).

meas. 5:   Cts. 1–2: Roll through foot, lowering into second position.

meas. 6:   Cts. 3–4: Shift lt., ending with R point tendu side, close front in fifth position.

meas. 7:   Cts. 5&6: Battement tendu R side, tendu relevé.

meas. 8:   Cts. 7–8: Close R back in fifth position demi-plié (L5) and straighten (M5).

meas. 9–16: Cts. 1–16: Sagittal reverse of meas. 1–8.

Battement Tendu #3:

Advanced level

Music: Andante Duple #2

Fifth position R front (rt. 2nd):

meas. 1:   Cts. 1–2: R slow battement tendu front.

meas. 2:   Cts. 3–4: Roll down through foot into "false" fourth (i.e., R leg non-weight-bearing), roll up through foot, returning to point tendu front.

meas. 3:   Cts. 5–6: Roll down through foot to fourth position [weight-bearing] with supports straight (M5), then shift weight back onto L with R point tendu front (2nd).

meas. 4:   Cts. 7–8: Close R into fifth position demi-plié and straighten.

meas. 5–8:   Cts. 1–8: Repeat meas. 1–4 to side, ending with R closing back in fifth position with arm movement remaining the same.

meas. 9–12:   Cts. 1–8: Repeat meas. 1–4 to back with arm movement remaining the same.

meas. 13:   Cts. 1–2: Demi-plié in fifth position (L5); keep supports bent but release heels from floor (M5).

meas. 14:   Cts. 3–4: Straighten supports into relevé [not a sous-sus] (H5).

meas. 15:   Cts. 5–6: Lower with straight supports into fifth position.

meas. 16:   Cts. 7–8: Demi-plié in fifth position and straighten (2nd).

meas. 17–32:   Cts. 1–32: Sagittal reverse of meas. 1–16.

Battement Tendu #4:

Intermediate level

Music: Polonaise

A very slow 3/4 with dancer's counts arranged in units of six.

Fifth position R front (rt. 2nd):

meas. 1:   Ct. 1: Battement dégagé R front on fondu.

Cts. 2–3: Straighten L support as R pulls into cou-de-pied front.

meas. 2:   Ct. 4: Roll through R foot into fifth position demi-plié with R front.

Ct. 5: Relevé with R cou-de-pied side.

Ct. 6: Demi-plié in fifth position with R back (L5).

meas. 3–4:   Cts. 1–2: Straighten R support and battement tendu L under (M5).

Cts. 3–4: Battement tendu L over (2nd).

Cts. 5–6: Demi-plié in fifth position and straighten.

meas. 5–8:   Cts. 1–12: Sagittal reverse of meas. 1–4, ending in fifth position with R front.

meas. 9–12:   Cts. 1–12: Repeat meas. 1–4 to side, ending in fifth position with R front (L5-M5) on ct. 6 of meas. 12.

meas. 13:   Cts. 1–2: Battement tendu R front (H5).

Ct. 3: Close R in fifth position (H5-palm changes in anticipation of arab. on 4th sixteenth note of ct. 3).

meas. 14:   Cts. 4–5: Battement tendu L back (arab.).

Ct. 6: Close L in fifth position (M5 on 4th sixteenth note of ct. 6).

meas. 15–16: Cts. 1–4: Battement tendu L over and under (arm moves slowly to 2nd).

Ct. 5: Demi-plié in fifth position (L5).

Ct. 6: Straighten.

Battement Tendu #5:

Intermediate level

Music: Schottische #1

Fifth position R front (rt. 2nd):

meas. 1: Cts. 1–2: Battement tendu R under (L5).

meas. 2: Cts. 3&4: Battement tendu L front (M5) and temps lié forward, ending R point tendu back (H5).

meas. &3: Cts. &5&6&: Close R fifth position back on "&," two more battements tendus back with accent *out* on the downbeat, closing on "&" of the beat.

meas. 4: Ct. 7: Battement tendu R back.

Ct. 8: Close in fifth position (2nd).

meas. 5–8: Cts. 1–8: Sagittal reverse of meas. 1–4, i.e., battement tendu R over, battement tendu L back, temps lié back with three battements tendus front, with arm movement remaining the same.

meas. 9–12: Cts. 1–8: Exact repeat of meas. 1–4.

meas. 13: Ct. 1: Fondu with R cou-de-pied back (L5-M5).

Ct. 2: Straighten L support with R retiré back (H5).

meas. 14: Cts. 3–4: Balance (lt. through M5 to H5).

meas. 15: Cts. 5–6: Press into sous-sus with R back.

meas. 16: Ct. 7: Demi-plié in fifth position (both 2nd with lt. regrasping barre).

Ct. 8: Straighten.

meas. 17–32: Cts. 1–32: Sagittal reverse of meas. 1–16.

Battement Tendu #6:

Beginning level

Music: Gavotte #2

First position (rt. H5):

meas. 1:	Ct. 1: Demi-plié in first position.
	Cts. 2–3: Battement tendu R front on fondu, straighten L support.
	Ct. 4: Close R in first position.
meas. 2:	Cts. 5–6: Battement tendu R front, close R in first position.
	Cts. 7–8: Demi-plié and straighten in first position (M5-2nd).
meas. 3–4:	Cts. 1–8: Repeat meas. 1–2 to side (L5-arab. cts. 7–8).
meas. 5–6:	Cts. 1–8: Sagittal reverse of meas. 1–2 to back (M5-2nd cts. 7–8).
meas. 7–8:	Cts. 1–3: Battement tendu R side and temps lié sideways, ending L point tendu side.
	Cts. 4–5: Demi-plié in second and temps lié sideways, ending R point tendu side.
	Ct. 6: Close R in first position.
	Cts. 7–8: Demi-plié in first position (L5) and straighten (arab.).
meas. 9–16:	Cts. 1–32: Sagittal reverse of meas. 1–8.

Battement Tendu #7:

Beginning level

Music: Gavotte #1

Fifth position R front (rt. 2nd):

meas. 1:	Ct. 1: Battement dégagé R side.
	Ct. 2: Flex ankle.
	Cts. 3–4: Demi-rond de jambe en dedans to front, keeping ankle flexed.
meas. 2:	Ct. 5: Point tendu R front.

Cts. 6–7: Temps lié forward, ending L point tendu back.

Ct. 8: Temps lié backward (demi-plié in fourth position).

meas. 3: Ct. 1: Complete the temps lié, ending R point tendu front.

Ct. 2: Close R front in fifth position.

Cts. 3–4: Battement tendu R under.

meas. 4: Cts. 5–7: Battement tendu R back, brush through first to battement tendu front, brush through first to battement tendu back.

Ct. 8: Close R back in fifth position.

meas. 5–8: Cts. 1–16: Sagittal reverse of meas. 1–4.

Battement Tendu #8:

Beginning level

Music: Andante Duple #1

First position (both arms forward and grasping barre):

meas. 1: Ct. 1: Battement tendu R side.

Ct. 2: Flex ankle.

Cts. 3–4: Rotate whole leg in and out.

meas. 2: Ct. 5: "Point" ankle.

Ct. 6: "Point" toes.

Cts. 7–8: Close R in first position demi-plié and straighten.

meas. 3: Cts. 1–2: Battement tendu R front and close in first position.

Cts. 3–4: Battement tendu R back and close in first position.

meas. 4: Cts. 5–7: Battement tendu R side and temps lié to side, ending L point tendu side.

Ct. 8: Close L in first position.

meas. 5–8: Cts. 1–16: Repeat meas. 1–4 to other side.

Battement Tendu #9:

Advanced level

Music: Tango

Fifth position R front (rt. 2nd):

meas. &1:   Ct. &1: Demi-plié in fifth position (L5), pivot 1/8 rt. on straightening L support with R battement tendu front (M5-H5).

               Ct. 2: Close R in fifth position.

meas. 2:   Cts. 3–4: Battement tendu R front and close in fifth position demi-plié.

meas. 3:   Ct. 5: Pivot 1/8 lt. on straightening L support with R battement tendu side (2nd).

               Ct. 6: Close R front in fifth position.

meas. 4:   Cts. 7–8: Battement tendu R side and close R back in fifth position demi-plié (L5).

meas. 5:   Ct. 1: Pivot 1/8 lt. on straightening L support with R battement tendu back (arab.).

               Ct. 2: Close R in fifth position.

meas. 6:   Cts. 3–4: Battement tendu R back and close in fifth position demi-plié (M5).

meas. 7:   Ct. 5: Pivot 1/8 rt. on straightening L support with R battement tendu side (2nd).

               Ct. 6: Close R back in fifth position.

meas. 8:   Cts. 7–8: Battement tendu R side and close front in fifth position demi-plié (L5).

meas. 9:   Ct. 1: Pivot 1/8 rt. on straightening L support with R battement tendu front (M5-H5).

               Ct. 2: Close R in fifth position demi-plié.

meas. 10:   Ct. 3: Pivot 1/8 lt. on straightening L support with R battement tendu side (2nd).

               Ct. 4: Close R back in fifth position demi-plié (L5).

meas. 11:   Ct. 5: Pivot 1/8 lt. on straightening L support with R battement tendu back (arab.).

               Ct. 6: Close R in fifth position demi-plié (M5).

meas. 12:   Ct. 7: Pivot 1/8 rt. on straightening L support with R battement tendu side (2nd).

Ct. 8: Close R front in fifth position demi-plié and straighten.

meas. 13–14:   Cts. 1–4: Port de bras forward (H5 in relation to spine) and return torso to vertical.

meas. 15–16:   Cts. 5–8: Cambré back and return torso to vertical.

Battement Tendu #10:

Advanced level

Music: A Sultry Tune

Fifth position R front (rt. 2nd):

meas. 1:   Ct. 1: Battement tendu R front (L5-M5-H5).

Ct. 2: Close R in fifth position.

Cts. 3–4: Battement tendu R under (2nd-L5).

meas. 2:   Ct. 5: Battement tendu L front (M5-H5).

Ct. 6: Close L in fifth position.

Ct. 7: Battement tendu L front.

Ct. 8: Release L from floor.

meas. 3:   Cts. 1–2: Tombé forward onto L [articulate through foot], ending in arabesque à terre on fondu (arab.).

Cts. 3–4: Tombé backward onto R [articulate through foot], ending L point tendu front on fondu (H5).

meas. 4:   Ct. 5: Draw L into sous-sus (M5).

Ct. 6: Release R to cou-de-pied back.

Ct. 7: Hold.

Ct. 8: Demi-plié in fifth position with R back.

meas. 5–8:   Cts. 1–16: Sagittal reverse of meas. 1–4.

ending chords: Straighten supports (2nd-L5).

BATTEMENT DÉGAGÉ DESCRIPTIONS

Arm movement indicated in parentheses is only for the right arm. Exceptions will be noted.

Battement Dégagé #1:

Intermediate level

Music: Polka #1

Fifth position R front (rt. L5):

meas. &1: Ct. &1: Battement dégagé R front and close in fifth position.

Ct. &2: Battement dégagé R under.

meas. &2: Ct. &3: Battement dégagé R back and close back in fifth position.

Ct. 4: Hold.

meas. &3: Ct. &5: Battement dégagé R back and close in fifth position.

Ct. &6: Battement dégagé R over.

meas. &4: Ct. &7: Battement dégagé R front and close in fifth position.

Ct. 8: Hold.

meas. &5: Cts. &1&2: Two battement dégagés front, closing in fifth position.

meas. 6: Ct. 3: Battement dégagé R front.

Ct. 4: Brush through first position to battement dégagé back.

meas. 7: Ct. 5: Brush through first position to battement dégagé front.

Ct. 6: Brush through first position to battement dégagé back on fondu.

meas. 8: Cts. 7&8: Pas de bourrée traveling forward, ending in fifth position demi-plié with R back.

meas. &9–16:   Cts. &1–16: Straighten L support with R battement dégagé back, sagittal reverse of meas. 1–8, but finish straightening supports in fifth position with R front.

Battement Dégagé #2:

Advanced level

Music: Polka #2

Fifth position R front (rt. 2nd):

meas. &1:   Ct. &1: Battement dégagé R front and close in fifth position.

Ct. 2: Hold.

meas. &2:   Cts. &3&4: Battement dégagé R under and over.

meas. &3:   Ct. &5: Battement dégagé L back.

Ct. 6: Hold.

meas. &4:   Cts. &7&8: Battement dégagé L over and under.

meas. 5:   Ct. 1: Fondu on L with R gesture cou-de-pied side (L5).

Ct. 2: Press to sous-sus with R back.

meas. 6:   Ct. 3: Fondu on R with L gesture cou-de-pied front.

Ct. 4: Straighten R support with L point tendu front (M5).

meas. &7–8:   Cts. &5&6&7: Release L from floor and battement dégagé three times front, closing in fifth on downbeat (slowly opens to 2nd).

Ct. 8: Hold fifth position with L front.

meas. &9–16:   Cts. &1–16: Sagittal reverse of meas. 1–8.

Battement Dégagé #3:

Intermediate level

Music: Polka #3

Fifth position R front (rt. L5):

meas. &1:   Cts. &1&2: Battement dégagé R two times front, closing in fifth position.

meas. &2: Cts. &3–4: Battement dégagé R under, hold.

meas. &3: Cts. &5&6: Battement dégagé R two times back, closing in fifth position.

meas. &4: Cts. &7–8: Battement dégagé R over, hold.

meas. &5: Cts. &1–2: Battement dégagé R under, hold.

meas. &6: Cts. &3–4: Battement dégagé L under, hold.

meas. &7–8: Cts. &5&6&7–8: Battement dégagé R under, over, under, hold.

meas. &9–16: Cts. &1–16: Battement dégagé R back, sagittal reverse of meas. 1–8 but finish in fifth position with R front.

Battement Dégagé #4:

Beginning level

Music: Polka #4

Fifth position R front (rt. L5):

meas. 1: Ct. 1: Battement dégagé R front.

Ct. 2: Close in fifth position.

meas. 2: Ct. 3: Fondu with R cou-de-pied front.

Ct. 4: Roll through R foot closing front in fifth position while straightening supports.

meas. 3: Cts. 5–6: Battement dégagé R under.

meas. 4: Ct. 7: Fondu with R cou-de-pied back.

Ct. 8: Roll through R foot closing back in fifth position while straightening supports.

meas. &5–6: Cts. &1&2&3: Battement dégagé R over, under, over, ending with R front in fifth position.

Ct. 4: Hold.

meas. 7: Cts. 5–6: Slow fondu on L with R cou-de-pied side.

meas. 8: Cts. 7–8: Roll through R foot closing back in fifth position while straightening supports.

meas. 9–16: Cts. 1–16: Sagittal reverse of meas. 1–8.

Battement Dégagé #5:

Intermediate level

Music: Slavic Duple

Fifth position R front (rt. 2nd):

meas. &1: Cts. &1–2: Battement dégagé R front and close in fifth position, hold.

Cts. &3&4: Two battement dégagés R front, closing in fifth position.

meas. &2: Cts. &5–6: Battement dégagé R under, hold.

Cts. &7&8: Battement dégagé R over, ballonné R under, ending R cou-de-pied back on fondu.

meas. &3: Cts. &1–2: Roll through R foot, closing back in fifth position demi-plié, straighten R and battement dégagé L under.

Cts. &3&4: Battement dégagé R under, ballonné R over, ending R cou-de-pied front on fondu.

meas. &4: Cts. &5–6: Roll through R closing front into fifth position demi-plié; straighten R and battement dégagé L over.

Cts. &7&8: Battement dégagé R over and under.

meas. &5–8: Cts. &1–16: Battement dégagé R back, sagittal reverse of meas. 1–4 but finish in fifth position with R front.

Battement Dégagé #6:

Beginning level

Music: Slavic Duple

First position (rt. 2nd):

meas. 1: Cts. 1–2: Battement dégagé R front, closing in fifth position.

Ct. &3: Battement dégagé R side, closing in first position.

Ct. &4: Battement dégagé R side, closing back in fifth position.

meas. 2: Cts. 5–6: Battement dégagé R back, closing in fifth position.

Ct. &7: Battement dégagé R side, closing in first position.

Ct. &8: Battement dégagé R side, closing front in fifth position.

meas. 3:   Cts. 1–3: Battement dégagé R front, brush through first position to battement dégagé back, brush through first position to battement dégagé front.

Ct. 4: Increase stretch of leg and raise slightly (allongé).

meas. 4:   Cts. 5–7: Brush through first position to battement dégagé back, brush through first position to battement dégagé front, brush through first position to battement dégagé back.

Ct. 8: Close R in first position.

meas. 5–8:   Cts. 1–16: Sagittal reverse of meas. 1–4.

Battement Dégagé #7:

Beginning level

Music: Polka #5

First position (both arms forward and grasping barre):

meas. &1:   Cts. &1–4: Battement dégagé R side four times, closing all front in fifth position.

meas. &2:   Cts. &5–8: Battement dégagé R side four times, closing all back in fifth position.

meas. 3:   Ct. 1: Battement dégagé R side on fondu.

Cts. 2&3: Pas de bourrée over, ending in fifth position demi-plié with R back.

Ct. 4: Relevé on L with R retiré back.

meas. 4:   Cts. 5–7: Balance (both hands off barre to M5).

Ct. 8: Demi-plié in fifth position with R back (regrasp barre).

meas. &5–8:   Cts. &1–16: Straighten R support and battement dégagé L side, repeat meas. 1–4 to other side, ending in fifth position with R front.

Battement Dégagé #8:

Intermediate level

Music: Polka #5

Fifth position R front (rt. 2nd):

meas. &1:   Cts. &1–3: R three ballonnés side [under, over, under], ending in fondu on the third ballonné with R cou-de-pied back.

             Ct. 4: Hold.

meas. &2:   Cts. &5&6: Coupé under, ending L cou-de-pied front; coupé over, ending R cou-de-pied back.

             Ct. 7: Straighten L support with R retiré side.

             Ct. 8: Close R front in fifth position.

meas. 3:   Ct. 1: Battement dégagé R front.

             Cts. 2&3: Brush through first position to battement dégagé back, battement dégagé front with third battement dégagé ending back.

             Ct. 4: Close R back in fifth position.

meas. 4:   Cts. 5–6: Retiré passé R front, closing front in fifth position.

             Ct. &7: Battement dégagé R side, closing in first position.

             Ct. &8: Battement dégagé R side, closing back in fifth position.

meas. &5–8:   Cts. &1–16: Battement dégagé R side (this is the beginning of the ballonné, which will close front), sagittal reverse of meas. 1–4, finishing in fifth position with R front.

Battement Dégagé #9:

Beginning level

Music: Polka #5

First position (both arms forward and grasping barre):

meas. 1:   Ct. 1: Battement dégagé R side.

             Ct. 2: Piqué [touch, release].

             Ct. 3: Piqué [touch, release].

meas. 2:   Ct. 4: Close in first position.

meas. 2:   Cts. 1–4: Exact repeat of meas. 1.

meas. 3:   Cts. 1–2: Battement dégagé R side, closing in first position.

Cts. 3–4: Battement dégagé R side, closing in first position.

meas. &4:   Cts. &5&6: Battement dégagé R side two times, closing in first position.

Cts. 7–8: Demi-plié in first position and straighten.

meas. 5–8:   Cts. 1–16: Repeat meas. 1–4 to other side.

Battement Dégagé #10:

Intermediate level

Music: Polka #6

Fifth position R front (rt. 2nd):

meas. &1:   Ct. &1: Battement dégagé R front, closing in fifth position.

Ct. &2: Battement dégagé R under.

meas. &2:   Ct. &3: Battement dégagé R back, closing in fifth position.

Ct. 4: Hold.

meas. &3:   Ct. &5: Battement dégagé R over.

Ct. &6: Battement dégagé R front, closing in fifth position.

meas. 4:   Ct. 7: Hold.

Ct. &8: Battement dégagé R under.

meas. &5–8:   Cts. &1–8: Sagittal reverse of meas. 1–4, finishing with R front in fifth position.

meas. &9–10:   Cts. &1–4: Battement dégagé R side four times, closing three in first position with the fourth closing back in fifth position.

meas. &11–12:   Cts. &5–8: Sagittal reverse with four battement dégagés side, closing three in first position with the fourth closing front in fifth position.

meas. &13–16:   Cts. &1–7: Battement dégagé R side seven times, closing six in first position with the seventh closing back in fifth position (port de bras slowly L5-M5-H5-2nd).

Ct. 8: Hold.

meas. &17–32:   Cts. &1–32: Sagittal reverse of meas. &1–16 with full en dedans port de bras on seven dégagés side, finishing the combination in fifth position with R front.

Battement Dégagé #11:

Advanced level

Music: Polka #5

Fifth position R front (rt. 2nd):

meas. &1:   Cts. &1&2: Battement dégagé R front two times, closing in fifth position.

Ct. &3: Battement dégagé R under.

Ct. 4: Fondu on L with R cou-de-pied side.

meas. 2:   Cts. 5–6: Press to sous-sus with R front, hold.

Ct. 7: Demi-plié in fifth position with R front.

Ct. &8: Changement.

meas. &3–4:   Cts. &1–8: Straighten L support and battement dégagé R back, sagittal reverse of meas. 1–2, finishing in fifth position with R front.

meas. &5–6:   Cts. &1–3: Battement dégagé R side three times, closing twice in first with the third closing back.

Ct. 4: Hold.

Cts. &5–7: Sagittal reverse of meas. 5–6, finishing with R front.

Ct. 8: Hold.

meas. 7:   Ct. 1: Battement tendu R side.

Ct. 2: Demi-plié in second position (M5).

Ct. 3: 1/2 pirouette en dehors to rt. (both M5).

Ct. 4: Remain on relevé with R retiré front (rt. 2nd grasping barre).

meas. 8:   Cts. 5–6: Lower R front to sous-sus (lt. to 2nd) and hold.

Ct. 7: Remain on relevé and battement dégagé L side.

Ct. 8: Demi-plié in fifth position with L front.

meas. &9–16:   Cts. &1–32: Straighten R support and battement dégagé L front, repeat meas. 1–8 to other side but straighten in fifth position on last count.

ROND DE JAMBE À TERRE DESCRIPTIONS

Arm movement indicated in parentheses is only for the right arm. Exceptions will be noted.

Rond de Jambe à Terre #1:

Intermediate level

Music: Lyrical Waltz #1

First position (rt. 2nd):

meas. 1: Battement tendu R front and demi-rond de jambe à terre en dehors, ending point tendu side.

meas. 2: Close in first position.

meas. 3: Battement tendu R side and demi-rond de jambe à terre en dehors, ending point tendu back.

meas. 4: Close in first position.

meas. 5–8: Three rond de jambes à terre en dehors, ending point tendu front.

meas. 9–10: Temps lié forward (L5-H5).

meas. 11–12: Brush L through first into grand battement front on fondu (arab.).

meas. 13: Press to rise, drawing L front into sous-sus (H5).

meas. 14: Stay relevé with R retiré back.

meas. 15: Balance (lt. to H5).

meas. 16: Demi-plié in fifth position with R back and straighten (both 2nd with lt. regrasping barre).

meas. 17–32: Sagittal reverse of meas. 1–16. Arms remain the same.

meas. 33–36: Battement tendu R side on fondu and port de bras into barre (H5 in relation to spine).

meas. 37–38:   Pivot [fouetté] 1/4 lt. to face barre, ending in lunge position with R point tendu back and torso folded over front (both hands grasping barre).

meas. 39–40:   Unfold torso to vertical as L support straightens.

meas. 41–42:   Lift R to arabesque.

meas. 43–44:   Body pulls away from barre (hands are supporting), ending with torso tilted forward and parallel to floor (arabesque leg has increased in height).

meas. 45–46:   Shift weight back to normal (back onto ball of support), bringing torso upright and keeping increased arabesque height.

meas. 47–48:   Fondu and relevé in arabesque (H5).

ending: Balance (lt. to H5).

Rond de Jambe à Terre #2:

Intermediate level

Music: Lyrical Waltz #2

Fifth position R front (rt. 2nd):

meas. 1–3:   Battement tendu R front and 2 1/2 rond de jambes à terre en dehors, ending point tendu back.

meas. 4:   Rond de jambe à terre en dedans (circle to point tendu front).

meas. 5–8:   Sagittal reverse of meas. 1–4, three rond de jambes en dedans, ending point tendu front and circle to point tendu back.

meas. 9–11:   Three rond de jambes à terre en dehors, finishing point tendu back.

meas. 12:   Brush R through first into grand battement front.

meas. 13–15:   Passé and développé back (M5-arab.).

meas. 16:   Close R back in fifth position (2nd).

meas. 17–32:   Sagittal reverse of meas. 1–16. Arms remain the same.

meas. 33–40:   Grand port de bras en dedans.

meas. 41:   Grand battement R front.

meas. 42–44:   Fouetté 1/2 lt., ending in arabesque (both M5-both 2nd with rt. grasping barre), fondu in arabesque (lt. to L5) on ct. 3 of meas. 44.

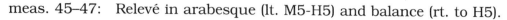

meas. 45–47: Relevé in arabesque (lt. M5-H5) and balance (rt. to H5).

meas. 48: Demi-plié, closing R back in fifth position (both 2nd with rt. regrasping barre), straighten.

meas. 49–64: Sagittal reverse of meas. 33–48, i.e., grand port de bras en dehors; grand battement back, rotation 1/2 rt., ending R grand battement front; relevé and close R front in fifth position demi-plié; straighten (both L5).

Rond de Jambe à Terre #3:

Intermediate level

Music: Lyrical Waltz #2

Fifth position R front (rt. 2nd):

meas. 1–4: Battement tendu R front and three rond de jambes à terre en dehors, ending point tendu front.

meas. 5: Rond de jambe à terre en dehors (circle to point tendu back).

meas. 6: Rond de jambe à terre en dedans (circle to point tendu front).

meas. 7–8: 1 1/2 rond de jambes à terre en dedans, ending point tendu back.

meas. 9: Brush through first to attitude front on fondu.

meas. 10–12: Remain on fondu and grand rond de jambe en dehors in attitude.

meas. 13: Relevé and extend to arabesque.

meas. 14: Remain in relevé and increase height of arabesque.

meas. 15: Close R back in fifth position demi-plié (L5).

meas. 16: Straighten in fifth position (M5-2nd).

meas. 17–32: Sagittal reverse of meas. 1–16.

meas. 33: Battement tendu R side.

meas. 34: Fouetté 1/4 lt., ending point tendu back (both forward and grasping barre).

meas. 35–36: Very deep fondu on L support as R slides out on toe (from top of head to R foot a diagonal line is created—center of gravity has moved backward).

meas. 37–40: Straighten L support with torso returning to vertical and center of gravity back to normal.

meas. 41–42: Lift R to arabesque.

meas. 43–44: Fondu and relevé arabesque.

meas. 45: Remain on relevé with chest rotating slightly lt. (H5).

meas. 46: (Lt. to H5).

meas. 47: Balance.

meas. 48: Demi-plié in fifth position with R back (both 2nd-both L5).

Rond de Jambe à Terre #4:

Intermediate level

Music: Lyrical Waltz #3

R point tendu back (rt. 2nd):

meas. 1–2: Two rond de jambes à terre en dehors, ending point tendu back.

meas. 3–4: Battement dégagé R front through first, then back through cou-de-pied side and extending dégagé height back.

meas. 5–8: Exact repeat of meas. 1–4.

meas. 9–12: 3 1/2 rond de jambes à terre en dehors, ending point tendu front.

meas. 13–14: Temps lié forward (L5-M5-arab.).

meas. 15–16: Temps lié backward (M5-2nd).

meas. 17–32: Sagittal reverse of meas. 1–16 using same arms ending R point tendu back.

meas. 33–36: Deep fondu on L support as R toe slides on floor.

meas. 37–38: Straighten L support (L5-M5-H5).

meas. 39–40: (2nd).

meas. 41: (L5).

meas. 42–44: Lift to arabesque (M5-arab.).

meas. 45–46: Fondu and relevé arabesque.

meas. 47–48: Balance in 2nd arabesque (release lt. into 2nd arab.).

Rond de Jambe à Terre #5:

Advanced level

Music: Lyrical Waltz #3

First position (rt. 2nd):

intro ct. 3: (L5).

meas. &1: Battement tendu R front on fondu (M5).

meas. 2: Straighten L and rond de jambe à terre en dehors to point tendu back (2nd).

meas. 3–4: Two rond de jambes à terre en dehors, ending point tendu back.

meas. 5–6: Battement dégagé R front and pass through cou-de-pied side, extending dégagé height back.

meas. 7–8: Two rond de jambes à terre en dehors, ending point tendu back.

meas. 9: Demi-plié croisé fourth position with R back (L5).

meas. 10: Relevé croisé fourth position (M5-H5).

meas. 11–12: Slowly shift weight onto L, lifting R into arabesque.

meas. 13–14: Balance (lt. to H5).

meas. 15: Demi-plié fifth position R back (lt. to 2nd regrasping barre/rt. to M5).

meas. 16: Straighten in fifth position (2nd).

meas. 17–32: Sagittal reverse of meas. 1–16.

meas. 33–39: Grand port de bras en dedans.

meas. 40: Demi-plié and sous-sus détourné 1/2 lt. (both M5 and at end of turn rt. to 2nd grasping barre).

meas. 41–47: Remain in sous-sus and grand port de bras en dehors.

meas. 48: Demi-plié (lt. to L5) and straighten in fifth position with L front.

Rond de Jambe à Terre #6:

Beginning level

Music: Lyrical Waltz #4

First position (rt. 2nd):

meas. 1:   Battement tendu R front and demi-rond de jambe à terre en dehors, ending point tendu side.

meas. 2:   Close first position.

meas. 3:   Battement tendu R side and demi-rond de jambe à terre en dehors, ending point tendu back.

meas. 4:   Close first position.

meas. 5–7:   Three rond de jambes à terre en dehors, ending point tendu back.

meas. 8:   Close first position.

meas. 9–16:   Sagittal reverse of meas. 1–8.

meas. 17–20:   Port de bras toward barre (H5 in relation to spine).

meas. 21–22:   Circle torso folded forward and low.

meas. 23–24:   Unroll [sequentially] torso to vertical (2nd).

meas. 25–28:   Port de bras toward barre (H5 in relation to spine).

meas. 29–30:   Circle to back.

meas. 31–32:   Return torso to vertical (2nd).

Rond de Jambe à Terre #7:

Intermediate level

Music: Lyrical Waltz #1

Fifth position R front (rt. 2nd):

meas. 1:   Battement tendu R front.

meas. 2:   Rond de jambe à terre en dehors to point tendu back.

meas. 3:   Battement tendu R through first to front.

meas. 4:   Rond de jambe à terre en dehors to point tendu back.

meas. 5–7:   Brush R through first and three rond de jambes à terre en dehors, ending point tendu back.

meas. 8:   Close R back into fifth position demi-plié (L5).

meas. 9:   Straighten L support with R retiré back (M5).

meas. 10:   Hold position (lt. to M5).

meas. 11–12:   Balance.

meas. 13–14:   (Both H5).

meas. 15:   Demi-plié in fifth position with R back (both to 2nd with lt. grasping barre).

meas. 16:   Straighten in fifth position.

meas. 17–32:   Sagittal reverse of meas. 1–16.

meas. 33:   Battement tendu R side.

meas. 34:   Lower R into second position.

meas. 35–36:   Fondu on R with L point tendu side.

meas. 37–38:   Port de bras side (lt. H5 in relation to spine/rt. L5 in relation to spine).

meas. 39–40:   Straighten R support and return torso to vertical (both M5-both 2nd).

meas. 41:   Pivot [rotation] 1/4 lt., ending with L point tendu front (both L5-both M5).

meas. 42:   Piqué forward onto L with R attitude back (both grasp barre).

meas. 43–46:   Balance (release rt. to H5 first, followed by lt. to H5).

meas. 47:   Close R back in sous-sus (both 2nd).

meas. 48:   Demi-plié in fifth position with R back (both L5).

Rond de Jambe à Terre #8:

Intermediate level

Music: Lyrical Waltz #2

Fifth position R front (rt. 2nd):

meas. 1–4:   Battement tendu R front and 2 1/2 rond de jambes à terre en dehors, closing R back in fifth position demi-plié (L5).

meas. 5–8:   Straighten L support and R battement tendu back (quickly M5-2nd), then 2 1/2 rond de jambes à terre en dedans, closing R front in fifth position demi-plié (L5).

meas. 9–10:   R retiré front on straight support (M5), hold.

meas. 11–12:   Fondu with R développé front.

meas. 13–14:   Demi-grand rond de jambe en l'air en dehors, straightening L support (2nd).

meas. 15:   Lower R to point tendu side.

meas. 16:   Close R back in fifth position.

meas. 17–32:   Sagittal reverse of meas. 1–16.

meas. 33:   Battement tendu R front.

meas. 34–36:   Fondu and port de bras forward over extended leg (H5 in relation to spine).

meas. 37–38:   Lengthen torso and return it to vertical with L support straightening.

meas. 39–40:   Battement tendu R back through first (2nd) (L5) on ct. 3 of meas. 40.

meas. 41:   (M5-H5).

meas. 42–44:   Cambré back.

meas. 45–46:   Return torso to vertical.

meas. 47–48:   Battement tendu R front through first position (2nd).

ending: Glissade forward (L5-M5-H5) sur les demi-pointes and balance in sous-sus R front (lt. to H5).

Rond de Jambe à Terre #9:

Advanced level

Music: Lyrical Waltz #1

Fifth position R front (rt. 2nd):

intro ct. 3:   (L5).

meas. 1:   Battement tendu R front on fondu (M5-H5).

meas. 2–3:   Remain on fondu and rond de jambe à terre en dehors, ending point tendu back (2nd-arab.).

meas. 4:   Straighten L support (M5-L5) and battement tendu R front through first (2nd).

meas. 5–8:   Four rond de jambes à terre en dehors, ending R point tendu front.

meas. 9:   Lift R grand battement height front.

meas. 10:   R retiré front.

meas. 11–12:   Port de bras toward barre (H5 in relation to spine).

meas. 13–14:   Demi-plié in fifth position with R front as torso folds forward (M5).

meas. 15:   Straighten L support and battement tendu R side (2nd).

meas. 16:   Close R fifth position back.

meas. 17–32:   Sagittal reverse of meas. 1–16 with identical arm movement. On ct. 3 of meas. 32, battement dégagé R front.

meas. 33–34:   Tombé forward onto R into a lunge and port de bras forward (H5 in relation to spine).

meas. 35–36:   Lengthen torso and return to vertical.

meas. 37–38:   Cambré back.

meas. 39–40:   Return torso to vertical (2nd).

meas. 41–42:   Shift weight forward onto straight R leg with L point tendu back (L5-arab.).

meas. 43–44:   Lift L into arabesque.

meas. 45:   Fondu arabesque.

meas. 46:   Relevé arabesque.

meas. 47–48:   Balance in arabesque (release lt. into 1st arab.).

Rond de Jambe à Terre #10:

Advanced level

Music: Lyrical Waltz #1

R point tendu back (rt. 2nd):

meas. 1:   Battement tendu R through first to front (L5-M5).

meas. 2:   Fondu and pulse (center of gravity down on ct. 1, center of gravity rises cts. 2–3).

meas. 3:	Center of gravity lowers again.
meas. 4:	Straighten L support and rond de jambe à terre en dehors, ending R point tendu back (2nd).
meas. 5–8:	Four rond de jambes à terre en dehors, ending point tendu back.
meas. 9:	Brush R through first into attitude front on fondu (L5-M5).
meas. 10:	Stay on fondu and demi-grand rond de jambe in attitude.
meas. 11–12:	Straighten L support and extend R side (2nd).
meas. 13–14:	Two rond de jambes en l'air en dehors, quickly pass through retiré side on ct. 3 of meas. 14.
meas. 15:	Développé R front on fondu.
meas. 16:	Straighten L support and lower R to point tendu front.
meas. 17–32:	Sagittal reverse of meas. 1–16 with identical arm movement.
meas. 33–34:	Fondu deeply with R toe sliding along floor.
meas. 35–36:	Port de bras forward (H5 in relation to spine).
meas. 37–40:	Lengthen torso and return to vertical.
meas. 41:	Battement dégagé R through first to front on fondu (2nd).
meas. 42:	Piqué forward onto R with L attitude back (L5-M5-H5).
meas. 43:	(Lt. H5).
meas. 44–46:	Balance.
meas. 47:	Demi-plié in fifth position with L back (both 2nd).
meas. 48:	Straighten supports in fifth position (both L5).

BATTEMENT FRAPPÉ AND FONDU DESCRIPTIONS

❧

Arm movement indicated in parenthesis is only for the right arm. Exceptions will be noted.

Battement Frappé and Fondu #1:

Intermediate level

Music: Polka #1

R point tendu side (rt. 2nd):

meas. &1:   Ct. &1: R cou-de-pied front with flexed ankle, battement frappé front.

           Ct. 2: Hold.

meas. &2:   Cts. &3&4: Two battement frappés side crossing front and back, ending demi-hauteur side.

meas. &3:   Ct. &5: Battement frappé front.

           Ct. &a6: Battement frappé double (royale), ending demi-hauteur back.

meas. &4:   Ct. &7: Battement frappé triple (entrechat six), beating back-front-back, ending demi-hauteur side.

           Ct. 8: Hold.

meas. &5–8:   Cts. &1–8: Sagittal reverse of meas. 1–4.

meas. &9–12:   Cts. &1–8: Repeat meas. 1–4 but relevé on ct. 8 of meas. 12 with cou-de-pied front (toes of gesture foot wrap underneath instep and heel is in front of support's heel). This cou-de-pied front position is assumed for all striking done in front when on relevé.

meas. &13–14:   Cts. &1–4: Remain on relevé and single battement frappé en croix.

meas. &15:   Cts. &5–6: Flic-flac en tournant en dedans pivoting 1/2 lt., ending with R cou-de-pied back (both M5-both 2nd with rt. grasping barre).

meas. 16:　Ct. 7: Close R back into sous-sus.

Ct. 8: Lower through straight R leg and point tendu L side.

meas. &17–32:　Cts. 1–32: Flex L cou-de-pied front and repeat meas. 1–16 to other side.

Battement Frappé and Fondu #2:

Intermediate level

Music: Polka #4

R point tendu side (rt. 2nd):

meas. &a1:　Ct. &a1: Battement frappé pointé (toe ends touching floor) double front.

Ct. 2: Hold.

meas. &a2:　Ct. &a3: Battement frappé pointé double back.

Ct. 4: Hold.

meas. &a3:　Ct. &a5: Battement frappé pointé double side.

Ct. 6: Hold.

meas. &4:　Cts. &7&8: Two battement frappés side.

meas. &5–8:　Cts. &1–8: Sagittal reverse of meas. 1–4.

meas. 9:　Ct. 1: Point tendu R side.

Ct. &2: Press to rise as R releases from floor, lower on straight leg with R touching floor.

meas. &a10:　Ct. &a3: Battement frappé pointé double (beat front-back) side.

Ct. &4: Rise and lower on straight support leg.

meas. &a11:　Ct. &a5: Battement frappé pointé double (beat back-front) side.

Ct. &6: Rise and lower on straight support leg.

meas. &a12:　Ct. &a7: Battement frappé pointé double (beat front-back) side.

Ct. &8: Rise and lower on straight leg.

meas. &13–15:　Ct. &1–6: Rise again, battement battu/serré cou-de-pied front (toes of gesture foot wrap underneath instep and heel is in front of support's heel) (L5).

meas. 16:   Ct. 7: Extend R side at demi-hauteur.

Ct. 8: Place in battement serré cou-de-pied front position.

Battement Frappé and Fondu #3:

Intermediate level

Music: March #1

Fifth position R front (rt. 2nd):

meas. 1:   Ct. 1: R cou-de-pied [pointed] front (L5).

Ct. &2: Point tendu R front on fondu (M5), demi-rond de jambe à terre en dehors as support straightens (2nd).

meas. 2:   Ct. 3: Cou-de-pied [pointed] front (L5).

Ct. &4: Point tendu R front on fondu (M5), relevé with R dégagé height side (2nd).

meas. &a3–4:   Cts. &a5–7: Battement frappé double three times side, always beating back-front (pointed cou-de-pied foot).

Ct. 8: Close R back in fifth position demi-plié.

meas. 5–8:   Cts. 1–8: Straighten L support and sagittal reverse meas. 1–4.

Battement Frappé and Fondu #4:

Intermediate level

Music: Coda

R cou-de-pied front with ball of ft. on floor (rt. L5):

meas. &1:   Ct. &1: Petit battement entrechat quatre (beating back and front) with ball of foot on floor.

Ct. 2: Battement frappé front.

meas. 2:   Ct. 3: Cou-de-pied front with ball on floor.

Ct. &4: Petit battement royale (beating front and back).

meas. &3:   Ct. &5: Petit battement entrechat quatre (beating front and back) with ball on floor.

Ct. 6: Battement frappé back.

meas. 4: Ct. 7: Cou-de-pied back with ball on floor.

Ct. &8: Petit battement royale (beating back and front) with ball on floor.

meas. &a5: Ct. &a1: Petit battement entrechat quatre (beating back and front) with ball on floor, then battement frappé front.

Ct. 2: Hold.

meas. &a6; Ct. &a3: Petit battement (beating front and back) with ball on floor, then battement frappé side.

Ct. 4: Hold.

meas. &a7: Ct. &a5: Petit battement (beating front and back) with ball on floor, with battement frappé back.

Ct. 6: Brush through first position, ending battement dégagé front on fondu.

meas. 8: Ct. 7: Draw R front into sous-sus and demi-détourné 1/2 to lt. (both M5-both 2nd with rt. grasping barre).

Ct. 8: Lower through straight R support as L is placed cou-de-pied front with ball on floor (lt. to L5).

Battement Frappé and Fondu #5:

Intermediate level

Music: Gavotte #1

Fifth position R front (rt. 2nd):

meas. 1: Ct. 1: Battement dégagé R front.

Ct. 2: Fondu with R cou-de-pied front (pointed foot).

meas. &2: Ct. &3: Chassé R through fifth position demi-plié (R non-weight-bearing]), then relevé with R battement dégagé side.

Ct. 4: Hold.

meas. &3–4: Cts. &5–7: Three single battement frappés side (pointed foot), crossing back-front-back.

Ct. 8: Close R back in fifth position demi-plié (L5).

meas. &5–8:   Ct. &1–8: (M5), sagittal reverse of meas. 1–4 (2nd on ct. 1 of meas. 5).

meas. 9–16:   Cts. 1–16: Repeat meas. 1–8, but all battement frappés are double. On final count, demi-plié in fifth position (L5) and straighten.

Battement Frappé and Fondu #6:

Beginning level

Music: Ragtime

Fifth position R front (rt. 2nd):

meas. 1:   Ct. 1: R cou-de-pied front (pointed foot).

Ct. 2: Flex ankle.

Ct. 3: Battement frappé front.

Ct. 4: Hold.

meas. 2:   Ct. 5: Cou-de-pied front (pointed foot).

Ct. 6: Flex ankle.

Ct. 7: Battement frappé side.

Ct. 8: Hold.

meas. 3–4:   Ct. 1: Cou-de-pied front with flexed ankle.

Ct. 2: Battement frappé front.

Ct. 3: Cou-de-pied front with flexed ankle.

Ct. 4: Battement frappé side.

Ct. 5: Cou-de-pied back with flexed ankle.

Ct. 6: Battement frappé back.

Ct. 7: Close R back in fifth position.

Ct. 8: Hold.

meas. 5–8:   Cts. 1–16: Sagittal reverse of meas. 1–4.

Battement Frappé and Fondu #7:

Intermediate level

Music: Schottische #1

R point tendu side (rt. 2nd):

meas. &1:   Ct. &1: Fondu with R flexed cou-de-pied front, straighten L and battement frappé front.

Ct. &2: Fondu with R flexed cou-de-pied front, straighten L and battement frappé side.

Cts. &3–4: Three rond de jambes en l'air en dehors at demi-hauteur.

meas. &2:   Cts. &5–8: Fondu with flexed cou-de-pied back, sagittal reverse of meas. 1–2.

meas. &3:   Cts. &1–4: Exact repeat of meas. 1 but relevé on ct. 2 and fondu with flexed cou-de-pied back on "&" of ct. 4.

meas. 4:   Ct. 5: Relevé with R demi-hauteur side.

Ct. &6: Fondu with cou-de-pied front with pointed foot (ballonné), relevé with R demi-hauteur side.

Ct. 7: Hold.

Ct. &8: Close R back in fifth position demi-plié, straighten L support and battement tendu R side.

meas. &5–8:   Cts. &1–16: Fondu with R flexed cou-de-pied back, sagittal reverse of meas. 1–4.

Battement Frappé and Fondu #8:

Intermediate level

Music: Adagio #7

R point tendu side (rt. 2nd):

meas. &1:   Release R from floor, fondu with cou-de-pied front (pointed foot) (M5).

meas. 2:   Straighten and extend demi-hauteur front.

meas. 3:   Fondu with cou-de-pied front (pointed foot).

meas. 4:   Straighten and extend demi-hauteur side (2nd).

meas. 5:   Fondu with cou-de-pied back (pointed foot) (L5).

meas. 6:   Straighten and extend demi-hauteur back (arab.).

meas. 7:   Fondu with cou-de-pied back (pointed foot) (M5).

meas. 8:   Relevé with R retiré back (H5).

meas. 9–12:   Balance (lt. L5 through M5 to H5).

meas. 13–14:   Lower R back into sous-sus.

meas. 15:   Demi-plié in fifth position R back (both 2nd with lt. regrasping barre).

meas. 16:   Battement tendu R side as L support straightens, R toe releases from floor on ct. 3 of meas. 16.

meas. &17–28:   Sagittal reverse of meas. 1–12.

meas. 29:   Lower R front into sous-sus.

meas. 30:   Demi-détourné 1/2 lt.

meas. 31:   Demi-plié in fifth position R back (both 2nd with rt. grasping barre).

meas. 32:   Battement tendu L side as R support straightens, L toe releases from floor on ct. 3 of meas. 32.

meas. 33–64:   Reverse repeat of entire combination but end straightening supports in fifth position with R front.

Battement Frappé and Fondu #9:

Beginning level

Music: Whirligig

Fifth position R front (rt. 2nd):

meas. 1:   Ct. 1: Cou-de-pied front (pointed foot).

Ct. 2: Fondu and flex R ankle.

Ct. 3: Straighten support and battement frappé front.

Ct. 4: Hold.

meas. &2:   Cts. &5–6: Two battement frappés front.

Ct. 7: Close R front in fifth position.

Ct. 8: Hold.

meas. 3–6: Cts. 1–16: Repeat meas. 1–2 to side and back.

meas. 7: Ct. 1: R retiré side.

Ct. 2: Hold.

Ct. 3: Close R front into fifth position, rolling through foot.

Ct. 4: Hold.

meas. 8: Cts. 5–6: Passé R and close fifth position back, rolling through foot.

Cts. 7–8: Passé R and close fifth position front, rolling through foot.

Battement Frappé and Fondu #10:

Advanced level

Music: Slavic Duple

R point tendu side (rt. 2nd):

meas. &1: Cts. &1–3: Flexed cou-de-pied front, three battement frappés side, alternating crossing gesture.

Ct. &4: Quick demi-rond de jambe en l'air (height lower than 45 degrees) en dedans to front and demi-rond de jambe en l'air en dehors to side.

meas. &2: Cts. &5–8: Sagittal reverse of meas. 1.

meas. &3: Cts. 1–4: Single battement frappé en croix, but finish fourth frappé side on fondu.

meas. 4: Cts. 5–6: Relevé and flic–flac en tournant en dedans pivoting 1/2 lt., ending R cou-de-pied back (both M5-rt. to 2nd grasping barre).

Ct. &7: Tombé onto R with L cou-de-pied front (pointed foot).

Ct. 8: Point tendu L side as R support straightens (lt. to 2nd).

meas. &5–8: Repeat meas. 1–4 to other side.

Battement Frappé and Fondu #11:

Beginning level

Music: Bright Waltz #1

R point tendu side (rt. 2nd):

meas. &1–2:	Release R from floor, battement fondu with R cou-de-pied front, then straighten support and extend R to point tendu front.
meas. 3–4:	Repeat battement fondu front but extend at demi-hauteur.
meas. 5:	Keep leg extended and flex ankle.
meas. 6:	Straighten L support with R demi-rond de jambe en dehors, keeping ankle flexed.
meas. 7:	Point foot.
meas. 8:	Lower to point tendu side, then release from floor on ct. 3 of meas. 8.
meas. 9–16:	Sagittal reverse of meas. 1–8.
meas. 17–24:	Battement fondu en croix at demi-hauteur.
meas. 25–28:	Lower to point tendu side, then port de bras toward barre (H5 in relation to spine).
meas. 29–30:	Lower R into demi-plié in 2nd (lt. releases barre) and temps lié rt., ending with L point tendu side (2nd). Torso slowly returns to vertical.
meas. 31:	Close L front in fifth position (both L5).
meas. 32:	Hold.

ROND DE JAMBE EN L'AIR DESCRIPTIONS

❧

Arm movement indicated in parentheses is only for the right arm. Exceptions will be noted.

Rond de Jambe en l'air #1:

Intermediate level

Music: Lyrical Waltz #3

Fifth position R front (rt. 2nd):

meas. 1: Battement dégagé R side.

meas. 2: Fondu with R cou-de-pied back.

meas. 3: Straighten L support and extend R demi-hauteur back.

meas. 4: Fondu with cou-de-pied back (L5), beat R cou-de-pied front on ct. 3 of meas. 4.

meas. 5: Straighten L support and extend demi-hauteur front (M5).

meas. 6: Fondu as R raises to hauteur (90 degrees).

meas. 7–8: Demi-grand rond de jambe en l'air en dehors as L support straightens (2nd), begin rond de jambe en l'air en dehors on ct. 3 of meas. 8.

meas. 9–11: Three rond de jambes en l'air en dehors, lower to tendu side on ct. 3 of meas. 11.

meas. 12: Lift side to hauteur (90 degrees).

meas. 13–14: Two double rond de jambes en l'air en dehors.

meas. 15: Lower to point tendu side.

meas. 16: Close R back in fifth position.

meas. 17–32: Sagittal reverse of meas. 1–16.

54

Rond de Jambe en l'air #2:

Intermediate level

Music: Big Waltz #1

Fifth position R front (rt. 2nd):

meas. 1:	Grand battement R side to hauteur (90 degrees).
meas. 2–4:	Three rond de jambes en l'air en dehors.
meas. 5:	Relevé with R retiré side (M5).
meas. 6–7:	Stay relevé and développé back (arab.).
meas. 8:	Close R back in fifth position demi-plié (2nd).
meas. 9–16:	Straighten L support and sagittal reverse of meas. 1–8. (On développé front rt. to H5.)
meas. 17–20:	Port de bras forward (H5 in relation to spine) and return torso to vertical.
meas. 21–24:	Cambré back and return torso to vertical (2nd).
meas. 25:	Demi-plié in fifth position R front (L5).
meas. 26:	Relevé with R grand battement side (M5-H5).
meas. 27:	Hold.
meas. 28–30:	Balance (lt. to H5).
meas. 31–32:	Close R front in fifth position demi-plié (both 2nd), straighten (both L5).

Rond de Jambe en l'air #3:

Intermediate level

Music: Lyrical Waltz #5

Fifth position sous-sus R front (rt. 2nd):

meas. 1:	Fondu with R cou-de-pied (pointed foot) front (L5).
meas. 2:	Straighten support and extend R front demi-hauteur (M5-2nd).
meas. 3–6:	Repeat meas. 1–2 side and back at demi-hauteur with first port de bras on each fondu and extension.

meas. 7:   Battement dégagé front on fondu.

meas. 8:   Demi-grand rond de jambe en dehors as L support straightens, begin rond de jambe en l'air en dehors on ct. 3 of meas. 8.

meas. 9–11:   Three rond de jambes en l'air en dehors.

meas. 12:   Close R back in fifth position sous-sus.

meas. 13–14:   Maintain sous-sus position but pull away from barre, allowing augmented chest area to fold over lt. surface (H5 in relation to spine).

meas. 15–16:   Return chest to vertical (2nd).

meas. 17–32:   Sagittal reverse of meas. 1–16.

Rond de Jambe en l'air #4:

Intermediate level

Music: Bright Waltz #4

Fifth position R front (rt. 2nd):

meas. 1:   Grand battement R side to hauteur (90 degrees).

meas. 2–4:   Two rond de jambes en l'air en dehors and close R back in fifth position.

meas. 5–8:   Sagittal reverse, ending R front in fifth position.

meas. 9–10:   Brush R to attitude front, brush through first to attitude back.

meas. 11–12:   Exact repeat of meas. 9–10.

meas. 13–14:   Raise attitude back.

meas. 15:   R point tendu back.

meas. 16:   Close R back in fifth position.

meas. 17–32:   Sagittal reverse of meas. 1–16.

Rond de Jambe en l'air #5:

Intermediate level

Music: Lyrical Waltz #6

Fifth position R front (rt. 2nd):

meas. 1:   Battement dégagé R front (allongé).

meas. 2:   Fondu with R cou-de-pied front (L5).

meas. 3:   Straighten support with R retiré front (M5).

meas. 4:   Développé R side (2nd), begin rond de jambe en l'air en dehors on ct. 3 of meas. 4.

meas. 5–8:   Three rond de jambes en l'air en dehors and close R back.

meas. 9–16:   Sagittal reverse of meas. 1–8.

meas. 17:   Battement dégagé R front (allongé).

meas. 18:   Fondu with R cou-de-pied front (L5).

meas. 19–24:   Repeat meas. 17–18 to side, back and side (M5-2nd when support straightens and leg extends), finishing R cou-de-pied front on fondu (L5).

meas. 25:   Relevé with R retiré front (M5).

meas. 26:   Hold.

meas. 27–30:   Balance (lt. to M5).

meas. 31:   (Both 2nd).

meas. 32:   Close R front in fifth position demi-plié (both L5) and straighten.

Rond de Jambe en l'air #6:

Intermediate level

Music: Lyrical Waltz #7

Fifth position R front (rt. 2nd):

meas. 1:   Battement dégagé R side (45 degrees), begin rond de jambe en l'air en dehors on ct. 3 of meas. 1.

meas. 2–3:   Two rond de jambes en l'air en dehors.

meas. 4: Lower to point tendu side.

meas. 5: Lift leg side to hauteur (90 degrees), begin rond de jambe en l'air en dehors on ct. 3 of meas. 5.

meas. 6–7: Two rond de jambes en l'air en dehors.

meas. 8: Close R back in fifth position.

meas. 9–16: Sagittal reverse of meas. 1–8.

meas. 17–20: Grand plié in fifth position (first port de bras), battement dégagé R side on fondu (allongé) on ct. 3 of meas. 20.

meas. 21: Relevé with R cou-de-pied back (L5).

meas. 22: Hold.

meas. 23–24: Close R back in fifth position demi-plié (M5) and straighten (2nd).

meas. 25–48: Sagittal reverse of meas. 1–24.

Rond de Jambe en l'air #7:

Advanced level

Music: Boston Waltz

Fifth position R front (rt. 2nd):

meas. 1: Grand battement R side to hauteur (90 degrees), begin rond de jambe en l'air en dehors on ct. 3 of meas. 1.

meas. 2–4: Three rond de jambe en l'air en dehors, R returns to retiré side (as if preparing to do another rond de jambe en l'air) on ct. 3 of meas. 4.

meas. 5–6: Développé front on fondu.

meas. 7: Straighten support as R brushes through first position to grand battement back.

meas. 8: Close R back in fifth position.

meas. 9–16: Sagittal reverse of meas. 1–8.

meas. 17–22: Exact repeat of meas. 1–6, but on ct. 3 of meas. 22 straighten support with R retiré side.

meas. 23–24: Développé back on fondu, straighten support with R retiré side on ct. 3 of meas. 24.

meas. 25–26: Développé side on fondu.

meas. 27:   Sous-sus with R front (L5-M5).

meas. 28:   Hold (lt. to M5).

meas. 29:   Demi-plié on ct. 1 of meas. 29, spring and sous-sus demi-détourné 1/2 lt. (both H5) on cts. 2–3 of meas. 29.

meas. 30:   Hold.

meas. 31:   Demi-plié in fifth position with L front (both M5).

meas. 32:   Straighten supports in fifth position (both 2nd with rt. grasping barre).

meas. 33–64:   Repeat entire combination to other side.

Rond de Jambe en l'air #8:

Advanced level

Music: Adagio #4

Fifth position R front (rt. 2nd):

meas. 1:   Grand battement R side to hauteur (90 degrees), begin rond de jambe en l'air en dehors on ct. 3 of meas. 1.

meas. 2–4:   Two rond de jambes en l'air en dehors and close R back in fifth position.

meas. 5–8:   Sagittal reverse of meas. 1–4, ending R front in fifth position (L5 when closing front in fifth).

meas. 9–10:   R retiré front (M5).

meas. 11–12:   Développé front on fondu (2nd), remain on fondu and point tendu R front (L5) on ct. 3 of meas. 12.

meas. 13:   Straighten support with R lifting to hauteur side (M5-H5).

meas. 14:   Hold.

meas. 15:   Point tendu R side (2nd).

meas. 16:   Close R back in fifth position.

meas. 17–32:   Sagittal reverse of meas. 1–16.

meas. 33–48:   Exact repeat of meas. 1–16, ending with R back in fifth position.

meas. 49:   Battement tendu R back.

meas. 50:   Rotation (turn into leg) 1/2 rt., keeping R à terre (lt. to H5/rt. 2nd grasping barre).

meas. 51–54: Fondu and port de bras forward, return torso to vertical with support straightening (lt. remains H5 in relation to spine).

meas. 55: Brush R through first position, ending point tendu back (2nd).

meas. 56: Lower to wide lunge position.

meas. 57–58: Remain in lunge and execute shallow port de bras forward, return torso to vertical (M5-H5).

meas. 59–62: Cambré back and return torso to vertical (2nd).

meas. 63: Straighten L support with R point tendu back.

meas. 64: Close R back in fifth position.

Rond de Jambe en l'air #9:

Intermediate level

Music: Lyrical Waltz #8

Fifth position R front (rt. 2nd):

meas. 1: Battement tendu R front.

meas. 2: Lift to attitude front.

meas. 3–4: Slow fondu with R remaining in attitude, but flex ankle (M5).

meas. 5–6: Straighten support as R extends front to battement height [press out with heel of foot, then point foot] (2nd).

meas. 7: Lower to point tendu front.

meas. 8: Close R front in fifth position.

meas. 9–16: Repeat meas. 1–8 to the back with L gesturing.

meas. 17–24: Repeat meas. 1–8 to side but lift R side to hauteur (90 degrees) on meas. 24; begin rond de jambe en l'air en dehors on ct. 3 of meas. 24.

meas. 25–30: Three rond de jambes en l'air en dehors immediately followed by three rond de jambes en l'air en dedans with third ending on fondu.

meas. 31: Close R front into sous-sus (M5), demi-détourné on cts. 2–3 (both M5-both 2nd with rt. grasping barre).

meas. 32: Demi-plié in fifth position with L front and straighten.

Rond de Jambe en l'air #10:

Advanced level

Music: Lyrical Waltz #8

Fifth position R front (rt. 2nd):

meas. 1: Battement dégagé R side, begin rond de jambe en l'air en dehors on ct. 3 of meas. 1.

meas. 2–3: Two rond de jambes en l'air en dehors with a fondu on the extension and straightening of the support when leg comes through passé, ending on fondu with leg side.

meas. 4: Close R back to fifth position with both supports straight.

meas. 5–8: Sagittal reverse of meas. 1–4.

meas. 9–12: Grand battement R side to hauteur (90 degrees) and execute three double rond de jambes en l'air en dehors.

meas. 13: Lower to point tendu side.

meas. 14: Lift side to hauteur, begin rond de jambe en l'air en dehors on ct. 3 of meas. 14.

meas. 15: Double rond de jambe en l'air en dehors.

meas. 16: Close R back in fifth position.

meas. 17–32: Sagittal reverse of meas. 1–16.

Rond de Jambe en l'air #11:

Advanced level

Music: Bright Waltz #4

Fifth position R front (rt. 2nd):

meas. 1: Brush R attitude front on fondu.

meas. 2: Close R front in fifth position with supports straight.

meas. 3–4: Repeat meas. 1–2 to side, closing R back in fifth position.

meas. 5: Sagittal repeat of meas. 1.

meas. 6: Straighten support with R retiré side (M5).

meas. 7:   Développé front on fondu.

meas. 8:   Demi-grand rond de jambe en l'air en dehors (leg no more than 90 degrees) on relevé (2nd), begin rond de jambe en l'air en dehors on ct. 3 of meas. 8.

meas. 9–12:   Four rond de jambes en l'air en dehors as support slowly lowers on taut leg.

meas. 13:   Draw R back to sous-sus (L5-M5-H5).

meas. 14:   Hold.

meas. 15:   Demi-plié in fifth position with R back (M5).

meas. 16:   Straighten (2nd).

meas. 17–32:   Sagittal reverse of meas. 1–16.

ADAGIO AND STRETCH DESCRIPTIONS

❧

Arm movement indicated in parentheses is only for the right arm. Exceptions will be noted.

Adagio and Stretch #1:

Advanced level

Music: Adagio #8

Fifth position R front (rt. 2nd):

intro ct. 3: (L5).

meas. 1: Battement tendu R front on fondu (M5).

meas. 2: Straighten support with R rond de jambe à terre en dehors to point tendu back (arab.).

meas. 3–4: Deep fondu on L with R toe sliding along floor (L5-back low).

meas. 5–6: Remain on fondu and lift to arabesque (back middle).

meas. 7–8: Straighten support as R changes to attitude back (H5).

meas. 9: R retiré side (M5).

meas. 10–12: Développé R front on fondu (2nd), step forward on R, lowering into demi-plié with L petit développé front (L5) on ct. 3 of meas. 12.

meas. 13: Piqué forward on L with R attitude back (M5-H5).

meas. 14–16: Balance in attitude (lt. to H5).

meas. 17–18: Promenade on relevé 3/8 lt. to end facing diagonally into barre (rt. to M5-rt. to 2nd grasping barre).

meas. 19–20: Extend R to arabesque (lt. back middle through L5 to arab.).

meas. 21–24: Penché arabesque and up, close R back into sous-sus on ct. 3 of meas. 24 (lt. to M5).

63

meas. 25–28: Remain on relevé and développé L side (lt. to H5).

meas. 29: Close L front in sous-sus (lt. to 2nd).

meas. 30: Fondu on L with R cou-de-pied back (lt. to M5).

meas. 31–32: Pas de bourrée under en tournant 3/8 to rt. (both M5-both 2nd with lt. grasping barre) and demi-plié in fifth position with R front, straighten (L5).

Adagio and Stretch #2:

Intermediate level

Music: Adagio #15

Fifth position R front (rt. 2nd):

intro ct. 3: (L5).

meas. 1–4: Développé R front (M5-H5).

meas. 5–8: Pass through retiré side and développé back (M5-arab.).

meas. 9–12: Pass through retiré and développé side (M5-H5).

meas. 13: Close R front into sous-sus (2nd).

meas. 14: Fondu on R with L cou-de-pied back (M5).

meas. 15: Pas de bourrée under en tournant 1/2 lt. (both M5-both 2nd with rt. grasping barre).

meas. 16: Close L front in fifth position demi-plié (lt. to L5) and straighten supports.

Adagio and Stretch #3:

Intermediate level

Music: Adagio #9

R point tendu front (rt. 2nd):

meas. 1: Increase tautness of R leg and release to dégagé height (allongé).

meas. 2: Fondu with R cou-de-pied front (L5).

meas. 3–4: Straighten L support and lift R to attitude front (M5).

meas. 5–6:   Développé front (H5).

meas. 7:   Lower to point tendu front (2nd).

meas. 8:   Demi-rond de jambe à terre en dehors, ending point tendu side.

meas. 9–16:   Repeat meas. 1–8 to side (open 2nd on développé).

meas. 17–24:   Saggital repeat of meas. 1–8 to back (arab. on développé), but in meas. 24 execute full rond de jambe en dedans, ending R point tendu front as support pivots 1/8 rt. facing away from barre (2nd).

meas. 25–28:   Fondu on L support with port de bras forward (H5 in relation to spine) and straighten support while returning torso to vertical.

meas. 29–32:   Cambré back, return torso to vertical (2nd) and close R front in fifth position (L5).

Adagio and Stretch #4:

Intermediate level

Music: Adagio #10

Face diagonally into barre with R leg front and supported on top of barre (rt. 2nd):

meas. 1–4:   Port de bras forward (H5 in relation to spine).

meas. 5–6:   Fondu with torso remaining folded forward.

meas. 7–8:   Straighten L support.

meas. 9–10:   Lengthen torso and return to vertical.

meas. 11–16:   Cambré back and return to vertical, quick fondu on ct. 3 of meas. 16.

meas. 17:   Relevé.

meas. 18:   Lift releasing leg from barre and hold.

meas. 19–22:   Grand rond de jambe en l'air en dehors (back diagonal middle-L5-arab.).

meas. 23–24:   Hold arabesque.

meas. 25:   Close R back into sous-sus (M5).

meas. 26–28:   Hold sous-sus (H5-2nd).

meas. 29–30:   Retiré L front (M5) and promenade 1/4 lt. (lt. M5 releasing barre/rt. arrives 2nd during promenade and grasps barre).

meas. 31–32: Développé L front and lower so it is supported on top of barre as R gradually lowers to flat (lt. M5 to 2nd).

Adagio and Stretch #5:

Beginning level

Music: Adagio #15

Face diagonally into barre with R leg front and supported on top of barre (rt. 2nd):

meas. 1–2: Port de bras forward (H5 in relation to spine).

meas. 3–4: Fondu and straighten.

meas. 5–6: Return torso to vertical (2nd on ct. 3 of meas. 6).

meas. 7–8: Fouetté 1/8 lt., ending with R to side on barre (both grasping barre).

meas. 9–10: Port de bras toward rt. side (lt. 2nd to H5 in relation to spine).

meas. 11–12: Fondu and straighten while torso remains curved rt.

meas. 13–14: Return torso to vertical (lt. to 2nd).

meas. 15: (Lt. to M5 grasping barre).

meas. 16: Press to rise.

ending chords: Lift and release leg from barre and hold.

Adagio and Stretch #6:

Intermediate level

Music: Adagio #15

Fifth position R front (rt. H5):

meas. 1–2: Fondu as R lifts to attitude front (M5 grasping inside of R heel with rt. hand).

meas. 3–4: Straighten support and extend leg side (2nd retaining grasp).

meas. 5–6: Rotate whole leg inward as torso tilts forward and center of gravity shifts backward.

meas. 7–8: Rotate leg outward as torso and center of gravity return to normal.

meas. 9–12: Repeat meas. 5–8.

meas. 13–14: Release grasp and hold leg side (stays 2nd).

meas. 15: Lower to point tendu side.

meas. 16: Close R front in fifth position (H5).

Adagio and Stretch #7:

Advanced level

Music: Adagio #11

Fifth position R front (rt. H5):

meas. 1–2: Fondu as R lifts to attitude front (M5 grasping inside of R heel with rt. hand).

meas. 3–4: Straighten support and extend leg front.

meas. 5–6: Demi-grand rond de jambe en l'air en dehors side (high 2nd retaining grasp).

meas. 7: Increase stretch (contract arm).

meas. 8: Hold stretch.

meas. 9–10: Fondu as R returns to attitude front.

meas. 11–16: Repeat meas. 3–8.

meas. 17–18: Retiré side (release and grasp inside of thigh).

meas. 19–20: Extend arabesque (back middle retaining grasp).

meas. 21–22: Penché arabesque.

meas. 23–24: (Release grasp-L5-arab.).

meas. 25–28: Return torso to vertical and hold arabesque.

meas. 29: Battement tendu R through first to front on fondu (L5-2nd).

meas. 30: Piqué forward onto R while pivoting 1/2 lt., closing L front in soussus at completion of turn (rt. M5-both 2nd with rt. grasping barre).

meas. 31–32: Demi-plié fifth position with L front and straighten (lt. L5 through M5 to H5).

meas. 33–64: Repeat meas. 1–32 on other side.

Adagio and Stretch #8:

Intermediate level

Music: Adagio #9

Face barre with R leg side and supported on top of barre (both forward and grasping barre):

meas. 1–2: Port de bras rt. (lt. to H5 in relation to spine).

meas. 3–4: Fondu and straighten.

meas. 5–6: Repeat fondu and straighten.

meas. 7–8: Return torso to vertical (lt. 2nd to M5 and grasp barre).

meas. 9–16: Repeat meas. 1–8 to other side with port de bras lt.

meas. 17–20: Center of gravity moves rt. causing R leg to slide along barre.

meas. 21–24: Slide back into balance on L support.

meas. 25–26: Fondu.

meas. 27–28: Relevé.

meas. 29–30: Lift and release leg from barre and hold side.

meas. 31–32: Close R in first position demi-plié and straighten supports (both L5).

Adagio and Stretch #9:

Intermediate level

Music: Adagio #9

Fifth position R front (rt. L5):

meas. 1–4: Développé R side (M5-H5).

meas. 5: Press to rise.

meas. 6: Tombé in place with L cou-de-pied back (2nd-M5).

meas. 7: Pas de bourrée under en tournant 1/2 lt. (both M5-both 2nd with rt. grasping barre).

meas. 8: Close L front in fifth position demi-plié (lt. 2nd to L5).

meas. 9–12: Straighten R support and développé L front (lt. M5 to H5).

meas. 13: Brush L through first position to arabesque (lt. arab.).

meas. 14:   Fondu arabesque.

meas. 15:   Pas de bourrée under in place (lt. to 2nd).

meas. 16:   Close L front in fifth position demi-plié and straighten supports
(lt. to L5).

meas. 17–32:   Repeat meas. 1–16 to other side.

Adagio and Stretch #10:

Intermediate level

Music: Adagio #9

Fifth position R front (rt. L5):

meas. 1–4:   Développé R side (M5-2nd).

meas. 5–6:   Rotation (turn into leg) 1/4 rt., ending with R leg front and
back to barre.

meas. 7–8:   Keep R front, continue pivot 3/8 rt. and end facing into barre
(lt. to H5/rt. grasps barre).

meas. 9–10:   Brush R through first position to attitude back (lt. M5 through L5
to 2nd, ending H5).

meas. 11–12:   Fondu on L and relevé in attitude.

meas. 13–15:   Remain in relevé and extend R arabesque (lt. M5 to arab.),
on ct. 3 of meas. 15, pivot 1/8 lt.

meas. 16:   Close R back in fifth position demi-plié and straighten
(lt. 2nd to L5).

meas. 17–32:   Repeat meas. 1–16 to other side.

Adagio and Stretch #11:

Intermediate level

Music: Adagio #9

Fifth position facing away from barre (rt. L5):

meas. 1–4:   Développé R front (M5-H5).

meas. 5–6:   Demi-grand rond de jambe en l'air en dehors (2nd).

meas. 7–8: Fouetté 1/4 lt. and finish facing diagonally into barre with R attitude back (H5).

meas. 9–10: Fondu in attitude.

meas. 11–12: Relevé attitude and hold.

meas. 13–14: R retiré side (M5).

meas. 15: Tombé in place with L cou-de-pied back and pas de bourrée under en tournant 1/2 lt., ending facing away from barre (both 2nd with rt. grasping barre).

meas. 16: Close L front in fifth position demi-plié and straighten (lt. to L5).

meas. 17–32: Repeat meas. 1–16 to other side.

Arm movement indicated in parentheses is only for the right arm. Exceptions will be noted.

Grand Battement #1:

Advanced level

Music: March #1

Fifth position R front (rt. 2nd):

meas. 1–2: Cts. 1–4: R two grand battements side, closing front and back (L5 on ct. 4).

meas. 3–5: Cts. 5–8,1–2: L grand battement three times front (M5-H5).

meas. 6: Ct. 3: Battement tendu L front.

Ct. 4: Demi-plié in fourth position (M5).

meas. 7–8: Ct. 5: Shift forward and relevé on L with R arabesque (arab.).

Cts. 6–7: Hold.

Ct. 8: Demi-plié in fifth position with R back (2nd).

meas. 9–16: Cts. 1–16: Sagittal reverse of meas. 1–8, but finish by straightening supports in fifth position with R front.

Grand Battement #2:

Intermediate level

Music: Big Waltz #4

Fifth position R front (rt. 2nd):

meas. 1–2: Grand battement R front and close in fifth position.

meas. 3–5: Grand battement R front, then brush through first to grand battement back (en cloche) and brush again (en cloche) through first to grand battement front.

meas. 6: Close R in fifth position.

meas. 7: Demi-plié in fifth position (L5).

meas. 8: Sous-sus (M5-H5).

meas. 9–14: Remain in relevé and grand battement R under, over, under.

meas. 15: Demi-plié in fifth position with R back (M5-L5).

meas. 16: Straighten supports (2nd).

meas. 17–32: Sagittal reverse of meas. 1–16.

Grand Battement #3:

Beginning level

Music: March #2

First position with back to barre (both side and grasping barre):

meas. 1: Ct. 1: R battement tendu front.

Ct. 2: Lift to hauteur (90 degrees).

Ct. 3: Lower to point tendu front.

Ct. 4: Close in first position.

meas. 2–3: Cts. 5–8, 1–4: Exact repeat of meas. 1, two more times with R gesturing.

meas. 4: Cts. 5–6: Grand battement R front and close first position.

Cts. 7–8: Repeat grand battement front, closing first position.

meas. 5–8: Cts. 1–16: Repeat above combination to other side with L gesturing.

Grand Battement #4:

Beginning level

Music: March #2

Fifth position R front (rt. 2nd):

meas. 1–2:   Cts. 1–6: R three grand battements front, closing in fifth position.

Cts. 7–8: R retiré passé, finishing back in fifth position.

meas. 3–4:   Cts. 1–8: Repeat meas. 1–2 side, finishing with R back.

meas. 5–6:   Cts. 1–8: Repeat meas. 1–2 back, finishing with R front.

meas. 7–8:   Cts. 1–8: Grand battement R en croix, finishing R front in fifth position.

Grand Battement #5:

Intermediate level

Music: March #3

Fifth position R front (rt. H5):

meas. 1–2:   Cts. 1–6: R grand battement front three times, closing in fifth position.

Cts. 7–8: Demi-plié in fifth position (M5) and straighten (arab.).

meas. 3–4:   Cts. 1–6: L grand battement back three times, closing in fifth position.

Cts. 7–8: Demi-plié in fifth position (M5) and straighten (2nd).

meas. 5–6:   Cts. 1–8: R grand battement four times side (under, over, under, over), ending front in fifth position.

meas. 7:   Ct. 1: Battement tendu R side.

Ct. 2: Demi-plié in fourth position with R back (M5).

Ct. 3: Relevé with R retiré front.

Ct. 4: Hold.

meas. 8:   Ct. 5: (Lt. to M5).

Cts. 6–8: Balance.

ending chords: Demi-plié in fifth position with R front and straighten
(both 2nd–both L5).

Grand Battement #6:

Intermediate level

Music: Big Waltz #4

Fifth position R front (rt. 2nd):

meas. 1–2:   R grand battement front and close fifth position.

meas. 3–4:   R grand battement under.

meas. 5–8:   Brush R to attitude back, brush through first to attitude front
(en cloche), brush through first to attitude back (en cloche)
and close R back in fifth position.

meas. 9–16:   Sagittal reverse of meas. 1–8, finishing with R front.

meas. 17–24:   R grand battement en croix, finishing with R front in fifth position.

meas. 25:   R battement tendu side.

meas. 26:   Demi-plié in second position.

meas. 27:   Shift to rt. and relevé on R with L retiré front (both M5).

meas. 28:   Demi-plié in fifth position with L front.

meas. 29:   Straighten L with R battement tendu back (2nd).

meas. 30:   Demi-plié in fourth position (L5-M5).

meas. 31–32:   Single pirouette en dehors (both M5), finishing in a lunge with
R back (2nd arab.).

Grand Battement #7:

Intermediate level

Music: March #1

Fifth position R front (rt. H5):

meas. 1:   Cts. 1–4: R grand battement front two times, closing in fifth
position (M5 on second closing).

meas. 2:   Cts. 5–6: R grand battement under (2nd-L5).

              Cts. 7–8: L grand battement front (M5-H5) and close front in fifth position.

meas. 3:   Cts. 1–4: R grand battement back (arab.) two times (M5 on second closing).

meas. 4:   Cts. 5–6: R grand battement over (2nd-L5).

              Cts. 7–8: L grand battement back (arab.) and close back in fifth position (H5).

Grand Battement #8:

Intermediate level

Music: Polonaise

A very slow 3/4 with dancer's counts arranged in units of six.

Fifth position R front (rt. 2nd):

meas. 1:   Ct. 1: R grand battement front.

              Ct. 2: Lower to point tendu front.

              Ct. 3: Lift front to hauteur (90 degrees).

meas. 2:   Ct. 4: Brush through first (L5) to grand battement back (arab.).

              Ct. 5: Lower to point tendu back.

              Ct. 6: Close R back in fifth position.

meas. 3–4:   Cts. 1–6: Sagittal reverse of meas. 1–2, finishing with R front (L5-2nd on grand battement through first to front).

meas. 5–6:   Cts. 1–6: R grand battement three times side (under, over, under).

meas. &7–8:   Ct. &1: Quick demi-plié in fifth position with R back (L5), relevé with R attitude back (M5-H5).

              Cts. 2–4: Hold.

              Ct. 5: Fifth position demi-plié with R back (2nd).

              Ct. 6: Straighten supports.

meas. 9–16:   Cts. 1–24: Sagittal reverse of meas. 1–8.

Grand Battement #9:

Advanced level

Music: Big Waltz #4

R point tendu back (rt. 2nd)

meas. 1–2:   R grand battement front (L5-M5-H5), then brush through first position to point tendu back (M5-L5-2nd).

meas. 3–6:   Repeat en cloche grand battement to point tendu back two more times, on ct. 3 of meas. 6 fondu L with R demi-rond de jambe en dedans side (slightly off floor).

meas. 7:   Assemblé soutenu en tournant en dedans [full revolution lt.] (both M5).

meas. 8:   Demi-plié in fifth position with R back (both 2nd with lt. regrasping barre).

meas. 9–14:   R grand battement side three times (over, under, over).

meas. 15:   Demi-plié in fifth position with R front (L5).

meas. 16:   Straighten L with R battement tendu front (M5-2nd).

meas. 17–32:   Sagittal reverse of meas. 1–16. On grand battement back, rt. arm swings 2nd-L5-arabesque and on brush to battement tendu front, rt. arm swings arabesque-L5-2nd. Assemblé soutenu en tournant will be en dehors.

Grand Battement #10:

Advanced level

Music: March #4

Fifth position R front (rt. 2nd):

meas. 1–2:   Cts. 1–6: R grand battement three times front with first two closing in fifth position and third finishing in cou-de-pied front on fondu (L5).

Cts. 7–8: Relevé with R passé (M5), ending in fifth position demi-plié with R back.

meas. 3–4: Cts. 1–8: Straighten L support and sagittal reverse of meas. 1–2, ending in fifth position demi-plié with R front. Arm movement is same as established in meas. 1–2.

meas. 5–6: Cts. 1–8: Repeat meas. 1–2 side, finishing in fifth position demi-plié with R front. Arm movement is same as in meas. 1–2.

meas. 7–8: Ct. 1: Straighten L with R battement tendu side (2nd).

Ct. 2: Demi-plié in second position (M5).

Ct. 3: 1/2 pirouette en dehors (both M5).

Cts. 4–5: Remain on relevé with R retiré front (rt. to 2nd grasping barre).

Ct. 6: Demi-plié in fifth position with R front.

Ct. 7: Straighten R and battement tendu L side (lt. to 2nd).

Ct. 8: Close L front in fifth position.

BALLET CENTER COMBINATIONS

Basil

Thompson

BIOGRAPHY

Basil Thompson was born in England, in Newcastle-on-Tyne, and studied dance from the age of nine. In 1951 he was awarded the Leverhulme Scholarship for three years of ballet studies at the Sadler's Wells Ballet School (the Royal Ballet). In 1954, Basil was one of 12 dancers chosen to join the Covent Garden Opera Ballet, where he danced featured roles in productions of *Carmen*, *Aida*, *The Tales of Hoffmann*, and *Le Coq d'Or*. He was promoted to the Sadler's Wells Ballet at Covent Garden in 1955 and toured with the company to the United States in 1955 and 1957.

Basil emigrated to the United States in 1958 and for two years taught ballet at the schools of Michel Panaieff, Eugene Loring, and David Lichine in Los Angeles.

In 1960, Basil joined American Ballet Theatre as a character dancer and assistant ballet master, and in 1969 he joined the Joffrey Ballet as ballet master, remaining with the company for 11 years.

Basil pursued a successful career as a freelance teacher, and in 1981 was invited by Ted Kivitt to join the Milwaukee Ballet as ballet master. During the 1986–87 season, he also acted as interim artistic director of that company, but following a joint venture with the Pennsylvania Ballet, he resumed his ballet master duties with the newly formed Pennsylvania/Milwaukee Ballet. Basil was also a senior teacher at the Milwaukee Ballet School.

After the dissolution of the Pennsylvania/Milwaukee Ballet venture in 1989, Basil became artistic director of the independent Milwaukee Ballet. In January 2000, he joined the faculty at the University of Iowa Dance Department.

INTERVIEW WITH BASIL THOMPSON

LC: *What teachers do you feel influenced you the most?*

BT: My earlier teachers, definitely. I had a teacher when I first went to the Royal Ballet School, Claude Newman [dancer with early Sadler's Wells], who was *extremely* sarcastic and *extremely* strict. I was terrified of him. In fact, I probably hated him at the time, but in later years I appreciated everything he told me. He insisted on exactitude. He was a stickler for doing all movements in the correct way, and he made us do them over and over again. Also, he was very insistent on students *knowing* what they were doing—the correct terminology. I stress even now among my own students the importance of knowing the correct terminology for the movement they are doing.

Another teacher, Harijs Plucis, was actually employed to be Margot Fonteyn's coach, but he also taught senior classes at the Royal Ballet School. I loved him; he was a great bear of a man, but very kind. He was from the old Russian school. His classes were very simple but strong—wonderful for building strength, particularly in male dancers.

Later on, I studied in New York with Bill Griffith [teacher at American Ballet Theatre and Joffrey Ballet]; he was extremely good on correct placement of the body, which helped my technique.

I would say that those three people were my main influences.

LC: *Did you also study with other teachers?*

BT: David Lichine [choreographer of *Graduation Ball*] who got me back into shape after a knee injury; Michel Panaieff [soloist with Original Ballet Russe]; Eugene Loring [dancer with American Ballet Theatre and choreographer of *Billy the Kid*]—these were all out on the West Coast. In Europe, Harold Turner [principal dancer with Sadler's Wells], Joan Lawson [teacher with Sadler's Wells]. Oh, there were many, many teachers: Igor Schwezoff [teacher at American Ballet Theatre] in New York, Stanislas Idzikowski [dancer with Diaghilev's Ballets Russes] in London . . .

LC: *Do you remember anything in particular that some of them gave you, some new insight perhaps, that made an impression on you?*

BT: Well, Idzikowski made an impression on my beats. He actually drew blood. But mind you, very kindly so. He made the point after the painful experience of trying to do entrechat six with street shoes on. . . . I always remembered to beat the legs, not the ankles.

LC: *He really had you wear street shoes?*

BT: Oh yes. The lesson stuck.

LC: *Do you feel that you stress one thing beyond all others in your teaching?*

BT: I try to remind students throughout the class to remember that it is a dancing class. I think students get very much tied up in the technical aspect of it. That's very good . . . but I think that sometimes they ignore the fact that it is not just physical prowess; it is dance. The two, I think, have to coordinate with each other. I admire the Russians for this because when I see their classes, particularly their higher classes, they accomplish what I would say is a whole body movement. It's not just the legs in the tendu and the feet pointed, but it's the coordination of the arms, the port de bras with it, the head, the feeling. I like to see even at the barre that it's not just barre work, but it's really dancing at the barre, particularly in more advanced classes.

LC: *Were you trained in any one specific method?*

BT: When I first started dancing, yes, I was taught the Royal Academy of Dancing syllabus and style. But then when I went to the Royal Ballet School, their syllabus was slightly different. It incorporated the strictness of the RAD, the port de bras of Cecchetti and also what the artistic director, Dame Ninette de Valois, of the Royal Ballet School wanted: a little of the Russian from her Diaghilev period.

LC: *As a teacher sometimes it's hard to find a balance between kindness and strictness. Students will react differently. Some will work very well for a teacher who is strict and others have a tendency to be turned off. Do you try to accommodate the different personalities?*

BT: Yes. You've got to know which ones you can drive and which ones would shy away if you got a little tough with them. You've got to be able to be a little considerate.

LC: *Do you have any other thoughts or concerns about dance that you'd like to tell me?*

BT: I don't know whether it is the present age, but I sometimes get the impression that students have the sense that the teacher is going to do everything for them. No doubt my teachers felt the same way.

❧

Battement Tendu and Pirouette #1:

Advanced level

Music: Lyrical Waltz #4

Fifth position croisé DSL (L5):

meas. 1–2: Battement tendu front croisé (M5/2nd) and close in fifth position.

meas. 3–4: Repeat tendu but close in fifth position demi-plié (2nd/M5).

meas. 5–6: 1 1/8 pirouettes en dehors (M5), ending DS point tendu back on fondu (2nd).

meas. 7–8: Pas de bourrée under, ending in fifth position with R front.

meas. 9–10: Battement tendu front, closing in fifth position demi-plié (rt. to M5).

meas. 11–12: 2 1/8 pirouettes en dehors (M5), ending DSR point tendu back in Russian 4th arabesque on fondu (Russian 4th arab.).

meas. 13–14: Straighten support.

meas. 15: (2nd).

meas. 16: Close R back in fifth position (L5).

Battement Tendu and Pirouette #2:

Intermediate level

Music: Lyrical Waltz #4

Fifth position DS with R front (L5):

intro ct.3: (M5).

meas. 1–2:   Battement tendu front (2nd) and close in fifth position.

meas. 3–4:   Battement tendu side and close in fifth position back (L5).

meas. 5:   R retiré side (M5).

meas. 6:   R point tendu front on fondu.

meas. 7–8:   Straighten support and rond de jambe à terre en dehors, ending point tendu back (2nd), demi-plié in fourth position (rt. to M5).

meas. 9–10:   Single pirouette en dehors (M5), ending in long fourth (2nd arab.).

meas. 11:   Pull up to point tendu back.

meas. 12:   Demi-plié fourth position (2nd/M5).

meas. 13–14:   Double pirouette en dehors (M5), ending in long fourth (2nd arab.).

meas. 15–16:   Pull up to point tendu back (2nd) and close R back in fifth position (L5).

Battement Tendu and Pirouette #3:

Advanced level

Music: Lyrical Waltz #9

Fifth position DS with R front (L5):

meas. 1–2:   Battement tendu front (M5) and close in fifth position demi-plié.

meas. 3:   Straighten L support with R retiré side and hold.

meas. 4:   Promenade 1/8 en dehors to DSR lifting to attitude back croisé (2nd/H5) and hold.

meas. 5–6:   Retiré side (M5) and lower to point tendu front effacé (H5/2nd).

meas. 7–8:   Tombé forward, pas de bourrée under (lt. to 2nd-L5), chassé L forward, ending point tendu back croisé (M5-2nd/H5).

meas. 9–12:   Temps lié backward with grand port de bras, ending point tendu front croisé (M5-H5/2nd-2nd-2nd/H5).

meas. 13–14:   Balançoire L into 1st arabesque (rt. through M5 to L5 and into 1st arab.).

meas. &15–16:   Fondu 1st arabesque, pas de bourrée under (2nd-rt. to L5) to fourth position demi-plié croisé (rt. to M5).

meas. 17–18:   Single pirouette en dehors (M5), ending in long fourth (croisé 2nd arab.).

meas. 19: Pull up to point tendu back croisé.

meas. 20: Demi-plié in fourth position croisé (2nd/M5).

meas. 21–22: Double pirouette en dehors (M5), ending in long fourth (croisé 2nd arab.).

meas. 23: Pull up to point tendu back croisé.

meas. 24: Demi-plié in fourth position croisé (2nd/M5).

meas. 25–26: Double pirouette en dehors (M5), ending attitude back croisé on fondu (2nd/H5).

meas. 27–28: Pas de bourrée under (rt. to 2nd) en tournant 3/4 rt., ending in long fourth croisé to DSL (rt. L5 to M5).

meas. 29–30: 2 1/4 pirouettes en dedans (M5) to end facing DSR with L on fondu and R cou-de-pied back (2nd).

meas. 31–32: Pas de bourrée back [back, side, back] en tournant 7/8 rt., ending DS in fifth position demi-plié with R back (L5).

Battement Tendu and Pirouette #4:

Advanced level

Music: Bright Waltz #4

Fifth position croisé DSL (L5):

intro ct. 3: (M5).

meas. 1–2: Battement tendu front croisé (H5/2nd) and close in fifth position.

meas. 3–4: Grand battement front croisé and close in fifth position.

meas. 5–6: R retiré side (2nd/M5), lower R to point tendu back effacé on fondu (rt. to H5).

meas. 7–8: Pas de bourrée under, ending fifth position demi-plié croisé (rt. to 2nd-L5).

meas. &9–12: (M5), repeat above meas. 1–4.

meas. &13: (Lt. to 2nd), chassé R forward to point tendu back croisé (L5-M5-2nd/H5).

meas. 14: Fondu to long fourth croisé (rt. to M5).

meas. 15: 2 1/4 pirouettes en dedans (M5).

meas. 16&: End DSR fifth position demi-plié croisé and straighten supports (2nd), (L5-M5).

meas. 17–32: Repeat meas.1–16 to the other side.

Battement Tendu and Pirouette #5:

Advanced level

Music: Bright Waltz #4

Fifth position croisé DSL (L5):

intro ct. 3: (M5).

meas. 1–2: Battement tendu back croisé (2nd/H5) and close in fifth position.

meas. 3–4: Grand battement back croisé and close in fifth position.

meas. 5–6: L retiré side, lower L to point tendu front effacé on fondu.

meas. 7–8: Pas de bourrée over (rt. to 2nd), ending in fifth position demi-plié croisé (L5).

meas. &9–12: (M5), repeat meas. 1–4.

meas. &13: Pivot on L 1/4 rt. to end facing DSR with R cou-de-pied side (rt. to 2nd), chassé backward onto R support, ending point tendu front croisé (L5-M5-2nd/H5).

meas. 14: Demi-plié fourth position croisé (rt. 2nd to M5).

meas. 15: Double pirouette en dehors (M5).

meas. 16&: Close R back in fifth position demi-plié croisé and straighten supports (2nd), (L5-M5).

meas. 17–32: Repeat meas. 1–16 to other side.

Grand Adagio #1:

Advanced level

Music: Adagio #8

Fifth position DS with rt. front (L5):

meas. 1-4: Développé R side (M5-2nd).

meas. 5:   R retiré side (M5).

meas. 6:   Pivot 1/8 lt. to DSL and développé front croisé on fondu (H5/2nd).

meas. 7–8:   Straighten support and balançoire R into 1st arabesque (lt. M5 to L5 then 1st arab.).

meas. 9–11:   En dedans promenade 5/8 lt. (M5-2nd arab. during promenade) to end facing SR.

meas. 12:   Fondu in 2nd arabesque.

meas. 13:   Piqué back onto R then assemblé soutenu en tournant en dehors 1 1/8 lt. (H5) to end facing DSR in croisé sous-sus.

meas. 14:   Hold sous-sus.

meas. 15–16:   Demi-plié in fifth position croisé (2nd) and straighten (L5).

meas. 17–18:   L retiré front (M5).

meas. 19–20:   Développé front croisé on fondu (2nd/M5).

meas. 21–23:   Straighten support and grand rond de jambe en l'air en dehors while pivoting 1/4 lt., ending in Russian 4th arabesque facing DSL (rt. to H5 to rt. back diagonal through L5 into Russian 4th arab.).

meas. &24:   Fondu, full pas de bourrée under en tournant lt. (2nd), ending DSL in fifth position demi-plié effacé (L5).

meas. 25–26:   Straighten R support with L retiré front (M5).

meas. 27–28:   Développé L into Russian 4th arabesque on fondu (Russian 4th arab.).

meas. 29–30:   Pas de bourrée under en tournant 1/8 rt. (2nd), ending DS in fifth position demi-plié with L front (L5).

meas. 31–32:   Straighten supports (M5-2nd), (L5).

Grand Adagio #2:

Intermediate level

Music: Adagio #8

Fifth position croisé DSL (L5):

meas. 1–2:   R retiré front (M5), point tendu front croisé on fondu.

meas. 3–4:   Glissade forward sur les demi-pointes (2nd/H5), hold sous-sus.

meas. &5:   (Rt. to 2nd), L pivot 1/8 rt. to face DS and fondu with R cou-de-pied front (L5).

meas. 6–8:   Straighten support and développé R side (M5-2nd).

meas. 9–12:   Retiré side (M5) and en dehors promenade 1/8 rt. to face DSR, lift to attitude back croisé (2nd/H5).

meas. 13–14:   Promenade 1/4 lt. to face DSL.

meas. 15–16:   Fondu 1st arabesque (1st arab.), pas de bourrée under (2nd) ending in fifth position demi-plié croisé (L5).

meas. 17–18:   Straighten L support with R retiré front while pivoting 1/8 rt. to face DS (M5).

meas. &19–20:   Pivot 1/8 rt. to DSR, développé front effacé (H5/2nd).

meas. 21–24:   Tombé forward, pas de bourrée under (lt. to 2nd) and chassé L forward, ending point tendu back croisé (L5-M5-2nd/H5) and hold.

meas. &25–28:   Fondu on L support and lower into lunge position (grand port de bras moving upstage and end 2nd/H5).

meas. &29–30:   (Rt. to 2nd-L5), straighten support in point tendu back croisé (M5-H5).

meas. 31–32:   Hold, close R back in fifth position croisé (2nd-L5).

Grand Adagio #3:

Advanced level

Music: Adagio #12

Fifth position DS with rt. front (L5):

meas. 1:   Cts. 1–2: R retiré front (M5), développé front on fondu.

    Cts. 3–4: Straighten support and promenade [fouetté] 1/4 lt., ending with leg in second facing SL (2nd), retiré side (M5).

meas. 2:   Cts. 5–6: Développé front.

    Cts. 7–8: Promenade [fouetté] 1/4 lt., ending with leg in second facing US (H5).

meas. 3:   Cts. 1–2: Promenade en dedans 1/2 lt. to DS.

    Cts. 3–4: Continue promenade 1/4 lt. into 1st arabesque to end facing SL (1st arab.).

meas. 4:   Cts. 5–6: Fondu 1st arabesque, pas de bourrée under 1/8 rt. (2nd) to DSL.

meas. 5: Cts. 7–8: Chassé R forward to point tendu back croisé (L5-M5) and lift L into Russian 4th arabesque (Russian 4th arab.).

meas. 5: Cts. 1–4: Full promenade en dedans in arabesque, fondu Russian 4th arabesque.

meas. 6: Cts. 5–6: Pas de bourrée under (2nd) 1/4 rt. to DSR, ending long fourth croisé (L5).

Cts. 7–8: Straighten L support and lift R to retiré side while pivoting 1/4 lt., ending DSL (M5), développé front écarté (2nd).

meas. 7: Cts. 1–2: Promenade 1/4 lt. into arabesque, ending USL, grand battement R front, fouetté temps levé (L5-M5-H5) to end facing DSR on fondu in croisé 1st arabesque (croisé 1st arab.).

Ct. 3: Step back onto R and balançoire L into 1st arabesque (L5-1st arab.).

Ct. 4: Hold 1st arabesque briefly, pas de bourrée under (2nd) with third step forward with R petit développé front (M5).

meas. 8: Ct. 5: Piqué forward onto R in 1st arabesque (L5-1st arab.) and hold, fondu 1st arabesque.

Cts. 6–8: Chassé en l'air en tournant 1/2 lt. toward USL (2nd) and tour jeté (L5-M5-H5-1st arab.), land facing DSR on fondu in 1st arabesque, piqué backward onto L and full assemblé soutenu en tournant en dedans, ending croisé sous-sus facing DSR (M5-H5/2nd); hold sous-sus.

Grand Adagio #4:

Intermediate level

Music: Adagio #8

Fifth position croisé DSL (2nd):

meas. 1–4: Grand plié (H5) and up (M5-2nd).

meas. &5: Demi-plié, spring to sous-sus (L5-Russian 4th arab.) and hold.

meas. 6–8: Continue holding sous-sus.

meas. &9: Demi-plié, spring to sous-sus détourné 3/4 lt. to end facing DSR (2nd-H5), (2nd ct. 3 of meas. 9).

meas. 10: Fondu on R with L cou-de-pied front (L5).

meas. 11–12: Straighten support and développé front croisé (M5-2nd/H5).

meas. 13–14: Balançoire L back into 1st arabesque (rt. M5 through L5 to 1st arab.) and hold.

meas. &15–16: Fondu 1st arabesque, pas de bourrée under (2nd) into fifth position demi-plié croisé (L5).

meas. &17: Chassé forward and lift R attitude back croisé (M5-2nd/H5).

meas. 18–20: Full promenade en dedans.

meas. 21–22: Retiré side (M5).

meas. 23–24: Développé front effacé (H5/2nd).

meas. 25–26: Tombé forward (lt. to 2nd), pas de bourrée under into fifth position demi-plié, then chassé forward on L, ending point tendu back croisé (L5-M5-2nd/H5).

meas. 27–30: Slow temps lié backward (grand port de bras moving upstage, ending 2nd).

meas. 31–32: (Allongé), close L front in fifth position croisé (L5).

Grand Adagio #5:

Advanced level

Music: Adagio #8

Fifth position croisé DSL (L5):

meas. 1–2: Battement dégagé front croisé on fondu (M5), straighten support and raise R at grand battement height écarté front (2nd/H5).

meas. 3–4: Promenade en dehors 1/4 rt. to DSR, R moves into attitude back croisé.

meas. 5–7: Promenade en dehors 3/4 rt. to end facing DSL (lt. to 2nd ct. 3 of meas. 7).

meas. 8: Extend to 1st arabesque (1st arab.).

meas. &9: Fondu 1st arabesque, pas de bourrée under (2nd), ending fifth position demi-plié croisé (L5).

meas. 10–11: Chassé forward (M5), straighten R support as L balançoire forward into effacé front (H5).

meas. 12–14: Promenade 3/8 rt. into second, ending in 1st arabesque facing SR (1st arab.).

meas. 15–16: Penché 1st arabesque.

meas. 17–18: Come up from penché.

meas. &19: Pivot 1/8 lt. to face DSR and failli L through into croisé long fourth (M5).

meas. &20–22: Petit développé R front and tombé forward (2nd); pas de bourrée under, ending fifth position demi-plié croisé (L5); chassé forward, ending point tendu back croisé (M5).

meas. 23–24: Fondu into croisé lunge (2nd/H5).

meas. 25–26: Port de bras forward (M5) and up (H5/2nd).

meas. 27–28: Cambré back and up (lt. to 2nd).

meas. 29: Draw R into sous-sus and hold (L5-M5-H5).

meas. &30–31: Pivot 1/4 lt. to face DSL and tombé forward onto L (2nd); pas de bourrée under, ending in croisé sous-sus [2nd step of pas de bourrée remains on relevé and R steps into croisé sous-sus]; détourné 3/4 lt. to face DSR (H5).

meas. 32: Hold sous-sus.

Grand Adagio #6:

Advanced level

Music: Adagio #10

Fifth position croisé DSL (L5):

intro ct. 3: Demi-plié in fifth position (M5).

meas. 1–2: Grand battement front croisé on relevé and hold (H5/2nd).

meas. &3–4: Tombé forward (2nd/L5), relevé on R in arabesque and hold (2nd/H5).

meas. 5: Fondu to croisé long fourth (rt. to 2nd).

meas. 6: (Rt. to M5).

meas. 7–8: 2 3/8 pirouettes en dedans in 1st arabesque (1st arab.), ending on fondu arabesque facing SR (H5/2nd).

meas. 9–10: Pas de bourrée under 1/8 lt. (lt. to 2nd) to face DSR, ending fourth position demi-plié croisé (M5).

meas. 11–12: Straighten L support and tendu R forward into effacé (H5/2nd).

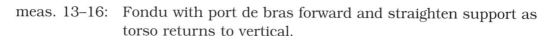

meas. 13–16:   Fondu with port de bras forward and straighten support as torso returns to vertical.

meas. &17–18:   (Rt. to L5), balançoire R back into croisé 2nd arabesque (croisé 2nd arab.), fondu croisé 2nd arabesque.

meas. 19–20:   Pas de bourrée under, en tournant (2nd) 3/4 rt. to DSL, ending on fondu R and L cou-de-pied back (L5).

meas. 21–22:   Step onto L and relevé with renversé en dehors (M5–H5) turning 1/4 rt. to DSR, ending in attitude back croisé on fondu (lt. to 2nd).

meas. 23–24:   Continue renversé movement in torso (windmill to H5/2nd) and pas de bourrée under en tournant (lt. to 2nd) 3/4 rt. to end facing DSL on fondu with L cou-de-pied back (L5).

meas. &25:   Deepen fondu while beating L to cou-de-pied front, développé front effacé (through attitude front) on relevé (M5-2nd/H5).

meas. 26–27:   Tombé forward on L (rt. to 2nd) and pas de bourrée under, ending croisé long fourth (rt. L5 to M5); straighten R support shifting forward into point tendu back croisé.

meas. 28:   Fondu, lowering into croisé long fourth.

meas. 29:   2 1/8 pirouettes en dedans in attitude back (H5/2nd) to end facing DS, fondu with L dégagé height side (lt. H5 to 2nd).

meas. 30:   Assemblé soutenu en tournant en dedans (M5) 1 1/8 rt. to DSR.

meas. 31–32:   Tombé forward onto R (2nd), pas de bourrée under, ending in fifth position demi-plié croisé, straighten (L5).

Relevé and Pirouette #1:

Advanced level

Music: Bright Waltz #3

Fifth position croisé DSL (L5):

intro ct. 3:   Fifth position demi-plié croisé.

meas. 1:   Sous-sus (M5-2nd/H5) and hold.

meas. 2–4&:   Demi-plié (H5/2nd), battement dégagé back croisé (M5) and pas de basque backward turning 1/4 rt. to DSR, ending point tendu front croisé (2nd); close in fifth position demi-plié croisé (L5); sissonne passée R forward, turning 1/8 rt. to face SR (M5).

meas. 5–7:   Tombé forward onto R (2nd) and pas de bourrée under into fourth position, then glissade forward, landing on R (L5); step L through and grand fouetté en dehors with temps levé turning 1/2 lt. to face SL (M5-H5).

meas. 8:   Land grand fouetté on L (1st arab.), relevé in 1st arabesque and hold (L5 on ct. 3).

meas. 9–11:   Tombé R forward and grand fouetté en dehors (M5-H5) with relevé turning 1/2 rt. to face SR (1st arab.); hold relevé in 1st arabesque after grand fouetté; pas de bourrée under turning 1/8 lt. to DSR (2nd), stepping forward on third step.

meas. &12:   Ballonné R over (M5).

meas. 13–14:   Piqué forward into effacé arabesque (H5/2nd) and hold, tombé L through, into croisé long fourth (lt. to 2nd).

meas. &15–16:   Petit développé R front (M5), tombé R forward (2nd) and pas de bourrée under to fifth position demi-plié croisé (L5).

Rond de Jambe à Terre and Pirouette #2:

Intermediate level

Music: Lyrical Waltz #4

Fifth position croisé DSL (L5):

meas. 1–4:   Battement tendu front croisé and three rond de jambes à terre en dehors, ending point tendu front croisé (M5-2nd/H5 during first rond de jambe).

meas. &5&6:   Temps lié forward and backward (M5), ending point tendu front croisé.

meas. 7–8:   Fondu and demi-rond de jambe en dehors to point tendu front écarté (2nd), straighten support and demi-rond de jambe en dehors to point tendu back effacé.

meas. &9–12:   Brush through first to begin 3 1/2 rond de jambes à terre en dehors, ending point tendu front croisé.

meas. 13–14:   R retiré side (rt. to M5), lower R back to fourth position demi-plié effacé.

meas. 15–16:   1 1/4 pirouettes en dehors (M5) to DSR, ending fifth position demi-plié croisé, straighten (2nd-L5).

Small Sauté #1:

Advanced level

Music: Polka #3

Fifth position demi-plié DS with R front (L5):

meas. &1–2:	Cts. &1–4: Three changement de pieds, sous-sus with L front.
meas. 3:	Cts. 5&6: Demi-plié in fifth position, changement battu (royale).
meas. 4:	Cts. 7–8: Sous-sus with R front, demi-plié in fifth position.
meas. 5–7:	Cts. 1–5: Repeat first 5 cts.
	Ct. &6: Entrechat quatre.
meas. 8:	Cts. 7–8: Straighten supports, demi-plié in fifth position with L front.

Small Sauté #2:

Advanced level

Music: Polka #3

Fifth position demi-plié DS with R front (L5):

meas. &1–2:	Cts. &1–4: Four changement de pieds.
meas. &3:	Cts. &5&6: Sissonne fermée over traveling rt. (low M5/low 2nd), sous-sus and demi-plié in fifth position with L front.
meas. &4:	Cts. &7–8: Sissonne fermée over traveling lt. (low 2nd/low M5), hold demi-plié in fifth position with R front (L5).
meas. &5–6:	Cts. &1–4: Four changement battus (royale).
meas. &7:	Cts. &5&6: Sissonne fermée over traveling rt. (low M5/low 2nd), sous-sus and demi-plié in fifth position with L front.
meas. &8:	Cts. &7–8: Sissonne fermée over traveling lt. (low 2nd/low M5), changement (L5), ending in fifth position demi-plié with L front.

Petit Allegro #1:

Advanced level

Music: Gavotte #2

Fifth position demi-plié DS with R front (L5):

meas. &1:   Cts. &1&2: Glissade to rt. without change (M5-L5), assemblé R under (allongé 2nd-M5).

Cts. &3&a4: Sissonne ouverte into 1st arabesque (1st arab.) turning 1/8 lt. toward DSL, pas de bourrée under turning 1/8 rt. (2nd), ending DS in fifth position demi-plié with R front (L5/low 2nd).

meas. &2:   Cts. &5&a6: Pas de chat traveling lt. (lt. M5 through H5 to 2nd), quickly flicking L to cou-de-pied back; pas de bourrée under to fifth position demi-plié with L front (rt. to M5).

Cts. &7&8: Brisé over traveling rt., temps de cuisse over traveling lt.

Petit Allegro #2:

Intermediate level

Music: Gavotte #2

Fifth position demi-plié croisé DSL (L5):

meas. &1:   Cts. &1&2: Glissade traveling forward (M5-2nd), changement de pieds en tournant 1/4 rt. to DSR (L5).

Cts. &3&4: Glissade traveling backward, changement de pieds en tournant 1/4 lt. to DSL.

meas. &2:   Cts. &5&a6: Straighten L support while pivoting 1/8 rt. to face DS and dégagé R side; tombé R side (M5-2nd) and pas de bourrée under, ending fifth position demi-plié with L front (L5).

Cts. &7–8: Assemblé over en tournant 1/8 lt. to DSL (2nd allongé-L5), hold demi-plié.

meas. &3:   Cts. &1&2: Glissade traveling forward (M5-2nd), changement de pieds en tournant 1/4 rt. to DSR (L5).

Cts. &3&4: Glissade traveling backward, entrechat quatre.

meas. &4   Cts. &5&a6: Straighten R support while pivoting 1/8 lt. to face DS and battement dégagé L side; tombé L side (M5-2nd) and pas de bourrée under, ending fifth position demi-plié with R front (L5).

Cts. &7-8: Assemblé over en tournant 1/8 rt. to DSR (2nd allongé-L5), hold demi-plié.

Petit Allegro #3:

Intermediate level

Music: Polka #7

Fifth position demi-plié DS with R front (L5):

meas. &1:   Ct. &1&: Two sautés in first position.

Ct. 2: Sauté into fifth position with L front.

meas. &2:   Cts. &3&4: Sissonne fermée forward turning 1/8 lt. to travel toward DSL (1st arab.), another sissonne fermée traveling toward DSL.

meas. &3:   Cts. &5&a6: Sissonne fermée over traveling to USL (2nd/M5); L cou-de-pied back and pas de bourrée under (rt. to 2nd) turning 1/8 rt. to DS, ending in fifth position demi-plié with L front (L5).

meas. &4:   Cts. &7&a8: Straighten L support while pivoting 1/8 rt. to face DSR and battement dégagé R front effacé (M5); tombé R forward (2nd) and pas de bourrée under, ending in fifth position demi-plié croisé (L5).

Petit Allegro #4:

Advanced-level preparation for Petit Allegro #5

Music: Tarantella

In this example, two counts are the equivalent of one measure of 6/8.

R on fondu with L cou-de-pied back facing DSL (2nd/M5):

meas. &a1:   Cts. &ua1–2: L piqué behind R turning 1/4 rt. to face DSR (rt. to 2nd), then R piqué side and lower into fondu (lt. to L5), chassé L forward and temps levé on L in croisé 1st arabesque (sweeping lt. forward into croisé 1st arab.).

meas. &a2: Cts. &a3–4: Repeat cts. &a1–2 on other side to DSL (2nd-sweep rt. from 2nd to L5 and forward into croisé 1st arab.).

meas. &a3: Cts. &a5–6: Repeat cts. &a1–2 but cabriole back and hold, landing in croisé 1st arabesque (2nd-sweep lt. from 2nd to L5 and forward into croisé 1st arab.).

meas. 4: Cts. 7&8: Pas de bourrée under (2nd) en tournant 1/4 lt. to face DSL, ending L cou-de-pied back (rt. to M5).

Petit Allegro #5:

Advanced level

Music: Tarantella

In this example, two counts are the equivalent of one measure of 6/8.

Fifth position demi-plié DS with R front (2nd):

meas. &1: Cts. &1&2: Glissade rt. without change, assemblé R under (allongé-M5).

meas. &2: Cts. &3&a4: Pas de chat [L begins pas de chat and travels lt., ending in fifth position with R front (lt. through H5 to 2nd/rt. to 2nd); L cou-de-pied back and pas de bourrée under to fifth position demi-plié with L front (M5).

meas. &3: Cts. &5-6: Three jetés over turning 7/8 rt. to end facing DSL (lt. to 2nd-M5/2nd-2nd/M5).

meas. &a4: Cts. &7–8: Pas de bourrée under to fifth position demi-plié effacé (rt. to 2nd-L5), chassé forward toward DSL and start temps levé on L in 1st arabesque (1st arab.).

meas. 5: Cts. 1&a2: Land temps levé in arabesque, R piqué behind L, then L piqué side and lower into fondu (2nd-rt. to L5); chassé temps levé forward on R in croisé 1st arabesque toward DSL (sweep rt. forward into croisé 1st arab.) and start temps levé.

meas. 6: Cts. 3&a4: Land temps levé in arabesque, pas de bourrée under turning 1/8 rt. (2nd) to face DS, ending in fifth position demi-plié with L front (L5).

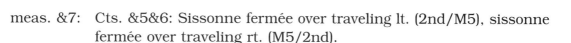

meas. &7:   Cts. &5&6: Sissonne fermée over traveling lt. (2nd/M5), sissonne fermée over traveling rt. (M5/2nd).

meas. 8:   Cts. 7–8: Straighten supports (lt. to 2nd), hold (L5).

Grand Allegro #1:

Advanced level

Music: Big Waltz #3

Croisé long fourth DSL (2nd):

intro cts. 2–3:   Demi-contretemps with en dedans rond de jambe gesture turning 1/4 rt. to DSR (M5).

meas. 1:   Step forward on R and cabriole back in 1st arabesque (L5-1st arab.).

meas. 2–4:   Step L through and glissade forward, landing on R (2nd); tombé L through and grand fouetté en dehors with temps levé turning 3/8 lt. to end facing SL in 1st arabesque (L5-M5-H5-1st arab.).

meas. &a5:   R piqué behind L turning 1/8 rt. to face DSL (2nd-L5), then L piqué side and lower into fondu; piqué forward onto R in croisé 1st arabesque (croisé 1st arab.).

meas. 6&a: Fondu croisé 1st arabesque, two steps in plié turning 1/2 lt. to face USR (2nd-L5).

meas. 7–8:   Step forward onto L and ballonné R side (2nd allongé), land ballonné with R cou-de-pied back (L5).

meas. &9:   Coupé under en tournant 3/8 rt. to end facing SL (M5), piqué forward on L into 1st arabesque (1st arab.).

meas. 10&a: Fondu 1st arabesque, chassé en l'air turning 1/2 rt. to face SR (2nd), step R forward.

meas. 11–12:   Tour jeté turning 1/2 rt. to end facing SL, landing on L in 1st arabesque (L5-M5-H5-1st arab.).

meas. &13–14:   Chassé en l'air turning 1/2 rt. to face SR (2nd) and step R forward; tour jeté turning 1/2 rt. to end facing SL, landing on L in 1st arabesque (L5-M5-H5-1st arab.).

meas. &15–16:   Pivot 1/4 rt. to face DS (2nd), piqué sideways onto R and assemblé soutenu en tournant en dedans to end facing DS in sous-sus with R front (M5); hold sous-sus (2nd/H5).

Ending Sauté #1:

Advanced level

Music: Schottische #2

Fifth position DS with R front (2nd):

meas. 1:   Cts. 1–4: Two grand battements under.

meas. 2:   Cts. &5&6&: Demi-plié in fifth position and four emboîtés en tournant [two full revolutions] clockwise traveling toward SR (lt. to M5 on first emboîté-2nd/M5-M5/2nd-2nd/M5), ending R cou-de-pied front.

Cts. 7: Cecchetti assemblé coupé, ending fifth position demi-plié with R front (L5).

Ct. &8: Entrechat six and straighten supports (M5-2nd).

Michael F.
Simms

BIOGRAPHY

Michael Simms is a native of St. Louis, Missouri, and received his early dance training with Stanley Herbertt of Ballet Theatre (now ABT). He has both performed and choreographed classical ballet and for musical theater and television. In St. Louis, Michael directed his own school, taught at Washington University, headed the dance program at Webster College and was artistic director of St. Louis Dance Theatre and Webster College Dance Theatre. In 1976 he moved to Columbia, Missouri, to join the dance faculty at Stephens College. After twenty years there, he took an early retirement to join his wife in Kansas City, where he became associate director of the Westport Ballet Theatre Company and School.

Michael has taught throughout the United States and in Europe and is in demand as a guest teacher and choreographer for regional ballet companies and university dance departments. In Europe he taught at the prestigious International Academy of Dance in Cologne, Germany, and in 1986 choreographed *No, No Nannette* at the Cork Opera House in Ireland. He has taught and adjudicated for many Association of Regional Ballet Festivals and Choreography Workshops.

Michael's students have gone on to become members of major ballet and modern dance companies, including American Ballet Theatre, the Royal Winnipeg Ballet, the Joffrey Ballet, the Miami Ballet, the National Ballet of Canada, the Hamburg Ballet, Bat-Dor, Les Grands Ballets Canadiens, the Martha Graham Company, and David Parsons Company. Others have become choreographers and dancers on Broadway.

Michael has studied the Bournonville technique of the Royal Danish Ballet under renowned Danish ballerina Toni Lander-Marks and has observed French school methods while attending classes at the Paris Opera Ballet and at the Rosella Hightower International School in Cannes, France.

Michael is proud to be serving on the dance panel for the National Foundation for Advancement in the Arts.

INTERVIEW WITH MICHAEL SIMMS

୧୧

LC: *Which teachers do you feel influenced you the most?*

MS: I'm like a sponge! The most influential would be my first teacher, Stanley Herbertt, who was trained by Edna McRae in Chicago. He was from Ballet Theatre in the 40s, long before it was American Ballet Theatre. He also studied all over the world with such notables as Olga Preobrajenska [prima ballerina of St. Petersburg Imperial Ballet] and Nora Kiss in Paris. Besides being a solo dancer with Ballet Theatre, he was also their principal character dancer, so he was much more than a technical teacher. He had a great deal to offer in both style and characterization. Because he toured as the soloist with *Carousel* and *Brigadoon*, he was very much influenced by musical theater and Agnes de Mille's choreography. He gave me a wonderfully diverse, complex range of styles and techniques—there was everything, from classical ballet to what was considered jazz at that time.

LC: *His technique wasn't reflective of one style, then? Was he like many Americans, who will take a little bit of this and a little bit of that; some English, some Danish, Russian . . .*

MS: He never defined what particular style or school he was training us in, although once in a while he would say, "This is the Cecchetti set" or the "Cecchetti *port de bras*," or he would say, "This is the Cecchetti manner of doing the cou-de-pied," and so forth. But I think that his was basically a Russian style; it certainly was not what I later learned is the "true English RAD" school when I went to Canada and studied the RAD technique. My teachers in Canada, Gweneth Lloyd and Betty Farrally [founders of Canadian School of Ballet in Winnipeg and Royal Winnipeg Ballet], were straight from England.

Later there were Winifred Edwards [principal teacher at the Royal Ballet School] and Betty Davies [principal teacher and examiner for the Royal Academy of Dancing] from the RAD. I think a certain amount of that RAD work is good for an advanced student. Actually I wasn't all that advanced; but I was ready for all that clarity and definition, which I find stifling to very young students trained in that method. To some extent the Cecchetti system is the same, but I now feel it is probably the best for youngsters.

LC: *What about the Bournonville technique? When and why did you get involved in learning more about this style?*

MS: The thing that has always attracted me to the Bournonville school and manner is the fleetness. It seems like excessive épaulement until you're doing it; then it feels very natural. It's as if I were a Danish dancer in another life. Fortunately I studied with Toni Lander [ballerina of the Royal Danish Ballet and American Ballet Theatre] the year before she passed away. She was absolutely divine as a person, divine as a dancer, and equally divine as a teacher. I think everybody who knew her felt something very special in their hearts about her and missed her terribly. She was very kind, very encouraging and very thorough. One of the highlights of that session was bringing *her* teacher, Mrs. Petersen, to watch class to give her the "seal of approval." Of course she told Toni that the class looked wonderful and she was teaching perfectly authentically. But it was the hardest thing to do physically that I have ever experienced in my life—you definitely do *not* want to begin Bournonville at 40 years old, as I did! Particularly the exercises in the class when you do changements from grand plié and changements to grand plié. We counted something like two hundred grand pliés in that class, and now that we've discovered that grand plié is so bad for you, I try to do the minimum in class. They put a lot of stress on the knees, and there are other ways to loosen up the hip, knee and ankle joints.

LC: *I know Rochelle Zide-Booth [ballerina with Ballet Russe de Monte Carlo, Joffrey Ballet and New York City Opera Ballet], for one, simply refuses to do grand pliés anymore.*

MS: None at all?

LC: *From when I last took class with her, I don't remember doing many—perhaps only in first and second position.*

MS: She's a wonderful teacher and I respect her highly.

LC: *What about the Russian influence?*

MS: I have had very little that was defined as Vaganova. One of the greatest influences in my life was Mme Maria Swoboda [principal teacher at the Ballet Russe School]. I feel very privileged to have worked with her. I don't think that she knew what she was teaching; she had the most phenomenal innate sense about conducting a class and setting combinations so that they made perfect kinesthetic sense to the dancer. I've never felt as warm and "on my legs" and as ready to dance as when I left the barre in her class. I know that a lot of what she gave me was based on the Vaganova school, especially the use of the back and the épaulement and the transitions. The transitions were very Russian, although not heavy at all as you sometimes see in the Russian school.

A lot of what I do now, in the adagio particularly, is based on what I felt Mme Swoboda gave me. Her adagios were very good for getting you on your legs with a lot of relevé. Not the sustained relevés in which you feel like a flamingo on one leg forever, but wonderful, fluid transitions. The combination that I give with the développé, relevé, développé, relevé, passé, développé, fondu is representative of her influence.

I have had so many wonderful teachers. Eric Braun [dancer with Ballet Theatre] was one, and I took his classes whenever I could get to Chicago. Larry Long is one of the finest teachers—he's a very intelligent man and an intelligent and passionate teacher. Mme Valentina Pereyaslavek [teacher at the Ballet Russe School] was influential to some degree, and Igor Schwezoff [teacher at the Ballet Russe School] was to a small degree also—a very great teacher. And then there's Arnold Spohr, the director of the Royal Winnipeg Ballet, who I think is a wonderful teacher. I think my teaching reflects all of those people.

LC: *That takes me to the next question. Do you feel that you stress one thing beyond all others in your teaching?*

MS: Yes, épaulement and transitions. I think transitions are very important, and the way I set combinations reflects that—the kind of transitions where you have to definitely finish one thing before it will connect to the next. I stress pirouettes and petit allegro a great deal. I always feel cheated at Stephens College because the classes are only an hour and twenty minutes, and I often don't have time to do enough grand allegro. Maybe that's why I stress petit allegro so much . . .

LC: *Do you have any other thoughts about teaching in general that you'd like to impart?*

MS: Teaching is what I always wanted to do. I performed professionally and loved performing, but only stayed in a ballet company for half of a season. I left Winnipeg at 17 years of age because I knew I wanted to come back to St. Louis and teach.

LC: *That's quite an early age to make such a decision.*

MS: I *started* teaching at 17, but I'm very glad that I had that early performing experience with the Royal Winnipeg Ballet, St. Louis Municipal Opera and St. Louis Civic Ballet. Even after I started teaching, I was still performing. I performed in a lot of musical theater as well, which was important. American dancers need to have all of their options open. That's one of the reasons I believe in the beneficial aspects of dancing in college: We're giving students a well-rounded and comprehensive dance education as well as a comprehensive liberal arts education, so they have something to dance *about*. This kind of education gives them something that is natural and innate to them to think about and express in choreography. Ballet dancers can become a very rarefied breed.

LC: *Realistically speaking, most of our students are not going to become performers, but their liberal arts education may open up other avenues of interest—perhaps notation, therapy or history.*

MS: A lot of my students who are not going to dance professionally are going into expressive arts therapy, as well as into the areas that you mentioned, and those interested in teaching will take our Methods of Teaching course at Stephens College.

LC: *The problem, of course, is to find a place for them to do their teaching. Do many start out teaching part time at a local studio, school or at the college itself?*

MS: I hope that they will take every opportunity to gain that experience. My college degree is in elementary education and I learned that 90 percent of it is a variable of that. It's a matter of getting into the classroom and gaining the practical experience of conducting a class—finding out that a large portion of your day is simply spent maintaining order and keeping students focused! Fortunately, at Stephens we have a practicum program where those who are interested in teaching can teach for credit in the physical education program. You probably have the same thing here, don't you?

LC: *Yes, those taking Pedagogy classes here at the University will go into the lower level classes and practice-teach there.*

Battement Tendu and Pirouette #1:

Advanced level

Music: Lyrical Waltz #9

Fifth position croisé DSL (L5):

meas. 1–2: Battement tendu back croisé on fondu (M5), draw L into sous-sus (2nd).

meas. &3–4: Demi-plié in fifth position croisé (L5), chassé forward to point tendu back croisé (M5-H5/2nd), fondu arabesque à terre (Russian 4th arab.).

meas. 5–6: Hold fondu position (croisé 2nd arab.), straighten R support (H5/2nd).

meas. 7–8: Temps lié backward with torso folding forward (M5) and then lt. (2nd/H5), hold point tendu position and bring torso to vertical (H5/2nd).

meas. 9–10: Fondu in point tendu front croisé, straighten and close in fifth position croisé.

meas. 11–12: Fondu with battement tendu front écarté (lt. to 2nd), pivot 1/8 rt. as support straightens and close R back to end facing DS.

meas. &13–14: Demi-plié in fifth position (rt. to L5), relevé on L with R retiré side (rt. to M5), demi-plié in fifth position with R front.

meas. 15–16: Pirouette en dehors (M5) 1 1/8 rt. to DSR, closing R back in fifth position demi-plié croisé, straighten supports (2nd-L5).

Battement Tendu and Pirouette #1a:

Advanced level

Music: Lyrical Waltz #9

A variation of Battement Tendu and Pirouette #1 enchaînement.

Fifth position croisé DSL (H5/2nd):

meas. 1–8: Repeat first eight measures of Battement Tendu and Pirouette #1, but close R into fifth position croisé on meas. 8 when torso returns to vertical (H5/2nd).

meas. &9–10: Two battement tendus front croisé with accent in.

meas. &11&12: Pivot 1/8 rt. to face DS with R battement tendu side, closing front with accent in (lt. to 2nd), battement tendu under with accent in (L5).

meas. &13–14: L petit développé side (M5-2nd) with fondu on R with 1/8 pivot lt. to face DSL, pas de bourrée under 1/4 rt. to face DSR, ending in fourth position demi-plié croisé (rt. to L5 then M5).

meas. 15–16: Relevé with R retiré front (or pirouette) (M5), close R back in fifth position demi-plié croisé, straighten supports (2nd-L5).

Grand Adagio #1:

Advanced level

Music: Adagio #8

Second position facing DS (2nd):

meas. 1–4: Grand plié in second position and straighten supports (L5-M5-2nd).

meas. &5–8: Shift lt. with R point tendu side and close in first position, grand plié in first position and straighten (L5-M5-2nd).

meas. 9–10: Wrap R cou-de-pied front and raise to retiré front (L5-M5).

meas. 11–12: Développé R front in fondu (2nd).

meas. 13–14: Posé forward onto R with L attitude back (lt. to L5 through M5 to H5/rt. M5 to 2nd) and hold.

meas. 15–16:   Extend into 2nd arabesque (2nd arab.).

meas. 17–18:   Begin grand rond de jambe en dedans (2nd).

meas. 19–20:   Pivot 1/8 lt. to face DSL as leg continues grand rond de jambe en dedans, ending front effacé (M5).

meas. 21–22:   Posé forward onto L into 1st arabesque (1st arab.) and hold position.

meas. 23–24:   (2nd-2nd arab.).

meas. 25–26:   Fondu arabesque (2nd/H5).

meas. 27–28:   Relevé arabesque, tombé R through, ending with L cou-de-pied back (rt. to 2nd).

meas. 29–30:   Pas de bourrée under turning 1/4 rt. to face DSR, ending on fondu with R cou-de-pied back (lt. to M5).

meas. &a31:   Pas de bourrée under turning 7/8 rt. to DS, ending in fifth position demi-plié with R front (lt. to 2nd-L5).

meas. &32:   Straighten R support and battement tendu L side (M5-2nd), lower L into second position.

Grand Adagio #2:

Advanced level

Music: Adagio #13a

In this example, two counts are the equivalent of one measure of 6/8.

Fifth position croisé DSL (L5):

meas. 1–2:   Cts. 1–4: Développé front croisé (M5-H5/2nd).

meas. 3:   Cts. 5–6: Retiré side (lt. to 2nd) and hold (M5).

meas. 4:   Cts. 7–8: Promenade 1/8 rt. to DS, développé side (2nd/H5).

meas. 5–6:   Cts. 1–3: Full promenade en dehors.

Ct. 4: Demi-grand fouetté en dehors 1/4 lt. to SL, ending in 2nd arabesque (2nd arab.).

meas. 7:   Cts. 5–6: Fondu 2nd arabesque, piqué backward onto R with L grand battement front (2nd/H5), grand fouetté en dehors 1/2 rt. to SR, ending in 1st arabesque (1st arab.).

meas. 8:　Cts. 7–8: Briefly hold relevé in 1st arabesque, pas de bourrée under (2nd) turning 1/8 lt. to DSR, ending in fifth position demi-plié croisé (L5), straighten supports.

Grand Adagio #2a:

Advanced level—a continuation of Adagio #2

Music: Adagio #13a and #13b

In this example, two counts are the equivalent of one measure of 6/8.

Fifth position croisé DSL (L5):

meas. 1–8:　Cts. 1–16: Repeat measures 1–8 of Adagio #2, but pas de bourrée under finishes in croisé long fourth facing DSR (2nd-lt. to M5).

meas. &9:　Ct. &1: Demi-contretemps turning 1/4 lt. to face DSL with R rond de jambe en dedans gesture (rt. to M5), landing on R with L dégagé front; piqué onto L in 1st arabesque (L5-1st arab.) and hold.

Ct. &2: Quickly fondu and chassé R through, into relevé croisé first arabesque (arms sweep through L5 to croisé 1st arab.).

meas. 10:　Cts. 3–4: Fondu in croisé 1st arabesque, lower L into croisé long fourth (2nd/M5).

meas. &11:　Cts. &5–6: (rt. to 2nd), 1 1/4 pirouettes en dedans in arabesque (H5) 1 1/4 rt., ending DSR in 1st arabesque fondu (1st arab.).

meas. &a12:　Ct. &a7: Pas de bourrée under (2nd), ending fondu with R cou-de-pied back (lt. to M5).

Ct. &a8: Pas de bourrée under (rt. to M5) en tournant 3/4 rt., ending DSL in croisé long fourth (lt. to 2nd).

meas. &13–16:　Cts. &1–8: Repeat 8 counts of meas. &9–12 to other side, but on last pas de bourrée en tournant finish DSR in fifth position demi-plié croisé and straighten supports (L5).

Grand Adagio #3:

Advanced level

Music: Adagio #13a and #13b

In this example, two counts are the equivalent of one measure of 6/8.

Fifth position croisé DSL (2nd):

meas. 1–2:   Cts. 1–4: Grand plié and straighten supports (L5-M5-2nd).

meas. &3:   Cts. &5–6: Fondu on L while pivoting 1/4 rt. to DSR with R petit développé front (L5), piqué 1st arabesque (1st arab.), chassé L through first to grand battement front croisé (L5-M5-H5) with relevé and grand fouetté en dehors 1/2 rt. to USL, ending in fondu 1st arabesque (1st arab.).

meas. 4:   Cts. 7–8: Straighten support and lower L to point tendu back with cambré back and focus to ceiling (lt. back low/rt. lifts very high to ceiling); torso to vertical and begin temps lié backward (lt. L5 to M5/rt. M5).

meas. 5:   Cts. 1–2: Finish temps lié backward, ending R point tendu front (H5/2nd), cambré back.

meas. 6:   Cts. 3–4: Return torso to vertical (lt. to 2nd-L5), fondu and lift R to grand battement height front (M5).

meas. 7–8:   Cts. 5–8: Straighten support and grand fouetté en dehors 1/2 lt. to DSR, ending croisé 2nd arabesque (H5-croisé 2nd arab.), close R back in fifth position croisé (L5).

meas. 9–10:   Cts. 1–4: Pivot 1/4 lt. to DSL and R développé front écarté (M5-2nd/H5), close R in fifth position croisé (rt. to 2nd).

meas. &11:   Cts. &5–6: Quick plié in fifth position (L5), relevé with pivot 1/4 rt. to DSR with R développé back écarté (M5-2nd/H5), close R back in fifth position demi-plié croisé (lt. L5/rt. 2nd to L5).

meas. &12:   Cts. &7–8: Relevé on L with 1/4 pivot lt. to DSL with R retiré side (M5) and hold, fondu with développé front croisé (H5/2nd).

meas. 13–14:   Cts. 1–4: Piqué forward into croisé attitude back, fondu on R support as L slowly lowers into croisé long fourth (2nd/M5).

meas. 15:   Cts. 5–6: 1 1/8 pirouettes en dedans in second (H5), ending DS; fondu on R with L dégagé height side (2nd); 1 1/8 assemblé soutenus en tournant en dedans ending DSR (M5).

meas. 16:   Cts. 7–8: Fifth position demi-plié effacé and chassé sideways
toward USR, ending point tendu front écarté (2nd-allongé),
close L front in fifth position croisé (L5).

Grand Battement, Chaîné and Pirouette (Relevé and Pirouette) #1:

Advanced level

Music: Bright Waltz #4

Fifth position croisé DSL (L5):

intro ct. 3:   (M5).

meas. 1–2:   Battement tendu front croisé (H5/2nd) and close in fifth position.

meas. 3–4:   Grand battement front croisé and close in fifth position.

meas. &5–7:   (Lt. to 2nd-L5), développé front croisé (M5-H5/2nd).

meas. 8:   Close in fifth position croisé (lt. to 2nd).

meas. &9:   Chassé L forward through first position, straighten L and pivot
1/4 rt. to face DSR with R demi-rond de jambe en dedans,
which ends point tendu front effacé (rt. through L5 to M5).

meas. &10–12:   Tombé R forward and begin clockwise chaîné turns (M5) moving
toward DSR, ending in fifth position effacé.

meas. 13:   Chassé forward to point tendu back effacé (H5/2nd).

meas. 14:   Close L back in fifth position effacé.

meas. 15–16:   Battement L into effacé arabesque on fondu, pas de bourrée
under (lt. to 2nd) to fifth position demi-plié croisé (L5-M5).

meas. 17–18:   Battement tendu under (H5/2nd) and close in fifth position effacé.

meas. 19–20:   Grand battement over (lt. 2nd to L5/rt. L5 on ct. 3 of meas. 20).

meas. 21–24:   Développé front écarté (M5-H5/2nd) and close back in fifth
position effacé (lt. to 2nd).

meas. 25–27:   Tombé R forward (lt. M5/rt. through L5 to M5) and begin
clockwise chaîné turns moving toward DSR, ending in fifth
position effacé.

meas. 28:   Hold fifth position.

meas. 29–30:   Chassé forward on R into effacé arabesque (H5/2nd),
pas de bourrée under (lt. to 2nd/rt. to L5) to fourth position
demi-plié croisé (rt. to M5).

meas. 31–32: Double pirouette en dehors (M5), ending in croisé long fourth (2nd).

Rond de Jambe à Terre and en l'air, Relevé Fouetté and Pirouette (Relevé and Pirouette) #2:

Advanced level

Music: Big Waltz #3

Fifth position DS with R front (L5):

meas. 1–3: Battement tendu front and two rond de jambes à terre en dehors (M5-2nd on first rond de jambe) with second one ending at grand battement height front croisé on fondu (L5-M5).

meas. 4: Straighten support with demi-grand rond de jambe en l'air en dehors (2nd).

meas. 5–6: Two rond de jambes en l'air en dehors.

meas. 7–8: Pivot 1/4 rt. on third rond de jambe en l'air, ending DSR with développé front effacé on fondu (lt. through L5 to M5).

meas. &9: Pas de basque sauté [leap to rt. side] (lt. to 2nd-L5), piqué forward onto L into croisé 1st arabesque (croisé 1st arab.) and hold relevé.

meas. 10–12: Fondu and chassé R through first to grand battement front (L5-M5-H5) and relevé into grand fouetté en dehors 1/2 lt. to USL (2nd), fondu and chassé R through (L5) to grand battement front (M5-H5) with relevé into grand fouetté en dehors 1/2 lt. to DSR, ending croisé 1st arabesque (croisé 1st arab.), hold relevé.

meas. 13: Close R back into croisé sous-sus (2nd).

meas. &14: Hold relevé and battement dégagé front croisé (rt. to L5), demi-plié fourth position croisé (rt. to M5).

meas. 15–16: Double pirouette en dehors (M5), ending in fifth position croisé (2nd).

Relevé and Pirouette #3:

Advanced level

Music: Polka #1

Fifth position demi-plié DS with R front (L5):

meas. &1: Cts. &1&2: Two échappés sur les demi-pointes changée (M5-2nd on first échappé), ending R front.

meas. &2: Cts. &3&4: Relevé with R retiré front (rt. through L5 to M5); demi-plié fifth position with R front; 1 1/8 pirouettes en dehors (M5) to DSR, ending in fifth position demi-plié croisé.

meas. &3: Cts. &5&6: Spring forward into sissonne (1st arab.) sur la demi-pointe pivoting 1/4 lt. to DSL, closing R back in fifth position demi-plié effacé; repeat sissonne sur la demi-pointe in 1st arabesque and close fifth position demi-plié effacé.

meas. &4: Cts. &7&8: Relevé pivoting 1/8 rt. to face DS with R retiré front (2nd/M5) and close R front in fifth position demi-plié; single pirouette en dehors (M5), closing R back in fifth position demi-plié; straighten supports (2nd).

Relevé and Pirouette #4:

Advanced level

Music: Bright Waltz #2

Fifth position DS with R front (L5):

intro ct. 3: (M5).

meas. 1: Battement tendu side (2nd).

meas. &2: Release R from tendu and pivot 1/8 rt. to DSR with demi-grand rond de jambe en l'air en dehors at dégagé height, demi-plié fourth position croisé (rt. to M5).

meas. 3–4: Single pirouette en dehors (M5), ending in croisé long fourth (2nd).

meas. &5–6: Petit développé R front (L5-M5), tombé R forward (2nd), pas de bourrée under, ending fourth position demi-plié croisé (rt. through L5 to M5).

meas. 7–8: Double pirouette en dehors (M5), ending in croisé long fourth (2nd).

meas. &9–11: Petit développé R front (M5), piqué 1st arabesque (1st arab.), fondu and chassé L through first to grand battement front (L5-M5-H5) with relevé into grand fouetté en dehors 1/2 rt., ending USL in 1st arabesque (1st arab.); fondu and chassé L through first to grand battement front (L5-M5-H5) with relevé into grand fouetté en dehors 1/2 rt., ending DSR in 1st arabesque on relevé (1st arab.).

meas. 12: Close L back in fifth position demi-plié effacé (M5), R steps rt. (2nd), petit développé L to point tendu front croisé (lt. through L5 to M5).

meas. 13: Tombé forward onto L into croisé long fourth.

meas. 14–16: 1 1/4 pirouettes en dedans (M5) to DSL; tombé onto R with L cou-de-pied back (2nd); pas de bourrée under en tournant 7/8 lt., ending DS with L front in fifth position demi-plié (L5); straighten supports.

Relevé and Pirouette #5:

Intermediate level

Music: Gavotte #2

Fifth position demi-plié DS with R front (L5):

meas. 1: Cts. 1–2: Sous-sus (M5) and demi-plié in fifth position.

Cts. 3–4: Straighten L support with R battement tendu side (2nd), step R back into fourth position demi-plié (rt. to M5).

meas. 2: Cts. 5–6: Single pirouette en dehors (M5), ending DS in long fourth (2nd).

Cts. 7–8: Straighten L support, ending point tendu back (allongé), close R back in fifth position (L5).

meas. &3–4: Cts. &1–8: Demi-plié in fifth position, repeat meas. 1–2 to other side.

meas. &5–6: Cts. &1–2: Fondu with R battement dégagé front and glissade forward sur les demi-pointes (M5), demi-plié in fifth position with R front.

Cts. 3–8: Exact repeat of cts. 3–8 in meas. 1–2.

meas. &7–8:   Cts. &1–8: Repeat meas. &5–6 to other side.

Relevé and Pirouette #6:

Intermediate level

Music: Bright Waltz #4

Fifth position DS with R front (2nd):

meas. 1–2:   Battement tendu R side, step R back into fourth position demi-plié (rt. to M5).

meas. 3–4:   Single pirouette en dehors (M5), ending R back in fifth position demi-plié.

meas. 5–6:   Straighten R support and battement tendu L side (2nd), step L back into fourth position demi-plié (lt. to M5).

meas. 7–8:   1 1/8 pirouettes en dehors (M5) to face DSL, ending in croisé long fourth (2nd).

meas. 9–10:   Full assemblé soutenu en dedans (L5), ending DSL in fifth position demi-plié croisé (M5).

meas. 11–12:   Straighten L support and battement tendu R front croisé (lt. to 2nd), lower R into croisé lunge.

meas. 13–14:   1 1/4 pirouettes en dedans (M5), ending DSR in croisé long fourth (2nd).

meas. 15–16:   Full assemblé soutenu en dedans (L5-M5-H5), ending DSR in fifth position demi-plié croisé (2nd).

Small Sauté #1:

Advanced level

Music: Polka #7

Fifth position croisé DSL (L5):

meas. &1:   Cts. &1&2: Sauté to second position turning 1/8 rt. to face DS (M5-2nd); sauté 1/8 rt. to DSR, ending fifth position demi-plié effacé (L5).

meas. &2:   Cts. &3&4: Sissonne passée front (end L cou-de-pied front) (2nd/M5), Cecchetti assemblé coupé.

meas. &3–4:   Ct. &5: Sissonne simple back (R cou-de-pied back) (M5/2nd).

           Cts. 6&7: Step R behind L (lt. to 2nd) and assemblé L under turning 1/4 lt. to face DSL (L5).

           Ct. &8: Changement de pieds en tournant turning 3/4 lt. to face DSR.

Petit Allegro #1:

Advanced level

Music: Allegro 6/8

In this example, two counts are the equivalent of one measure of 6/8.

Fifth position demi-plié DS with R back (2nd):

meas. &1:   Cts. &1&2: Two jetés over (rt. to M5-2nd/lt. to M5-2nd).

meas. &2:   Cts. &3&4: Glissade rt. without change (lt. to 2nd), jeté R over (rt. to M5).

meas. 3:   Cts. &5&6: Jeté L over (M5/2nd), temps levé.

meas. &a4:   Cts. &a7–8: Step R behind L with 1/8 pivot lt. to face DSL (lt. to L5); step L forward (lt. begins to move to arab./rt. to L5); brush R croisé front and assemblé traveling forward (Cecchetti 3rd arab.), ending in fifth position demi-plié croisé.

meas. &5:   Cts. &1–2: Petit développé L front (M5) and piqué to 1st arabesque (1st arab.), fondu 1st arabesque and chassé en l'air turning 1/2 rt. to end facing USR (2nd).

meas. 6:   Cts. 3–4: Step onto R and assemblé en tournant 1/2 rt. to end facing DSL without change (R ends front) (L5-M5-H5-2nd).

meas. &7:   Cts. &5&6: Sissonne over turning 1/8 rt. to DS (M5), sissonne ouverte forward (2nd/H5).

meas. 8:   Cts. 7–8: Pas de bourrée under (rt. to 2nd), ending in fifth position demi-plié with R front (L5).

Petit Allegro #2:

Intermediate level

Music: Mazurka #1

In this example, three counts are the equivalent of one measure of 3/4.

Variation A:

Ballonné composé de côté, described below in detail, is repeated on the diagonal until the dancer exits the stage area.

Fifth position demi-plié croisé DSL (2nd/H5):

intro ct. 6:   Ct. 6: Brush R side and hop.

meas. 1:   Ct. 1: Land hop with R cou-de-pied front.

Ct. 2: Chassé to R side.

Ct. 3: Step L behind R, then brush R side and hop.

Variation B:

Fifth position demi-plié effacé to DSR (2nd/H5):

meas. &1:   Cts. &1–3: Ballonné composé de côté traveling rt. toward USR.

meas. 2:   Cts. 4–6: When leaping into pas de basque sauté en avant (rt. to 2nd), turn 1/4 rt. in air to face USR (lt. through L5 to M5).

meas. 3:   Cts. &1–3: Ballonné composé de côté traveling lt. toward DSR (lt. to H5).

meas. 4:   Cts. &4–6: When leaping into pas de basque sauté en avant (lt. to 2nd), turn 1/4 lt. in air to face DSR (rt. through L5 to M5).

Continue repeating meas. 1–4 across the stage area. The ballonné and pas de basque are bigger [cover more space] in meas. 3–4 to facilitate traveling to DSR.

Variation C:

Fifth position demi-plié effacé to DSR (2nd/H5):

meas. &1–4:   Cts. 1–6, 1–6: Repeat above 4 meas. of Variation B, which ends facing DSR.

meas. 5:   Cts. 1–3: When leaping into pas de basque sauté en avant, turn 1/4 rt. in air (rt. to 2nd) to face USR (lt. through L5 to M5).

meas. 6:   Cts. 4–6: Full piqué turn en dedans (M5) to end facing USR (M5/2nd).

meas. 7:   Cts. 1–3: 1 1/4 assemblé soutenus en dedans (M5) to end facing DSR.

meas. 8:   Cts. 4–6: Fifth position demi-plié croisé.

meas. 9–16:   Cts. 1–6, 1–6, 1–6, 1–6: Repeat meas. 1–8 to other side.

Petit Allegro #3:

Advanced level

Music: Polka #3

The following two enchaînements were taught separately and then combined. Part I, which is performed on both sides, proceeds directly into Part II, which is also performed on both sides.

Part I:

Fifth position demi-plié DS with R back (L5):

meas. &1:   Cts. &1&2: Two jetés over.

meas. 2:   Cts. 3&4: Bournonville pas de bourrée couru traveling to SL with torso folded over rt. and head turned rt. (2nd/M5), jeté sideways to lt. with R ending dégagé height side (rt. to 2nd).

meas. 3:   Cts. 5&6: Bournonville pas de bourrée couru traveling to SL with torso folded over rt. and head turned rt. (rt. to M5), jeté sideways lt. with R ending cou-de-pied front while turning in air 1/8 lt. to face DSL (rt. to 2nd-L5).

meas. &4:   Cts. &7&8: Jeté forward, ending with L gesture attitude back croisé (M5-2nd); Cecchetti assemblé coupé (L5).

meas. &5–8:   Cts. &1–8: Repeat meas. 1–4 to other side. On ct. &1 turn 1/8 rt. in air to face DS.

Part II:

Fifth position demi-plié DS with R back (L5):

meas. &1:   Cts. &1&2: Two jetés over.

meas. &2:   Cts. &3–4: Step R behind L (M5) while pivoting 1/8 lt. to face DSL, step L forward, battement dégagé R forward and assemblé moving forward (H5/2nd), ending in fifth position demi-plié croisé.

meas. &3:   Cts. &5&6: L jeté over turning 1/8 in air to face DS (2nd/M5), temps levé battu.

meas. &a4:   Cts. &a7–8: Pivot on L support turning 3/8 rt. to face USR, step forward onto R, step L behind R (lt. to M5) and brush R front into jeté en tournant while turning 1/2 rt. to end facing DSL in attitude back croisé (H5/2nd).

meas. &5–8:   Cts. &1–8: Repeat meas. 1–4 to other side. On ct. &1 turn 1/8 rt. in air to face DS.

Petit Allegro #4:

Intermediate level

Music: Polka #7

Fifth position demi-plié DS with R back (2nd):

meas. 1–2:   Cts. &1–4: Three jetés over (rt. to M5-2nd/lt. to M5-2nd/rt. to M5), temps levé.

meas. 3:   Cts. &5–6: Glissade lt. without change (rt. to 2nd), ballonné L over (L5).

meas. 4:   Cts. 7–8: Step L in front of R (low M5), assemblé R over (L5-2nd-L5).

Grand Allegro #1:

Advanced level

Music: Grand Allegro Waltz

Point tendu croisé front DSR (2nd):

meas. 8&a:	Step forward onto L and glissade forward through fourth position, tombé L through, ending R cou-de-pied back (M5).
meas. 1:	Relevé with développé back écarté (2nd/H5).
meas. 2:	Close R front in fifth position demi-plié effacé (rt. to 2nd).
meas. &a3:	Rond de jambe L en dedans, tombé forward onto L with R petit développé front (M5), piqué forward onto R with L développé front croisé (2nd/H5).
meas. 4&a:	Tombé L forward (rt. to 2nd); glissade forward through fourth position; tombé L through, ending R cou-de-pied back (M5).
meas. 5–8:	Repeat meas. 1–4 but finish in croisé long fourth to DSR (rt. to 2nd).
meas. &9:	Demi-contretemps turning 1/4 lt. to face DSL with R gesture rond de jambe en dedans, land on R (M5), piqué on L in 1st arabesque (L5-1st arab.).
meas. 10&a:	Fondu in 1st arabesque, chassé back en l'air turning 1/2 rt. to face USR (2nd).
meas. 11–12:	Step forward onto R and tour jeté 1/2 rt., ending DSL in 1st arabesque (L5-M5-H5-1st arab.).
meas. &13:	Pivot 1/2 rt. to face USR (2nd), step forward onto R and cabriole back in 1st arabesque (rt. through L5 into 1st arab.).
meas. 14:	Tombé L to side and balancé en tournant 5/8 rt. to end DS (2nd/M5).
meas. &15:	Pivot 1/8 rt. to face DSR with R petit développé front (lt. to M5), temps levé in 1st arabesque (L5-1st arab.).
meas. 16&:	Step L forward, grand jeté développé (M5-Cecchetti 3rd arab.) landing on R with L tombé through, ending in croisé long fourth (2nd).

Grand Allegro #2:

Advanced level

Music: Running Duple

Point tendu croisé front DSL (L5):

meas. &1: Cts. &1&2: Pivot 1/4 rt. to face DSR, tombé R forward (L5-low M5), step L behind R and assemblé R under (L5-2nd-allongé-L5).

meas. &2: Cts. &3&4: Sissonne simple front (L ends cou-de-pied front), step forward on L (M5), step R behind and brush L front, assemblé front (2nd/H5).

meas. &3: Cts. &5&6: Sissonne simple back (R ends cou-de-pied back) turning 1/4 lt. to end facing DSL (rt. to 2nd-L5), chassé en l'air traveling backward (M5), battement dégagé R back and assemblé R back (2nd/H5).

meas. &4: Cts. &7&8: Sissonne ouverte traveling forward landing on L, tombé R through (rt. to 2nd), pas de bourrée under en tournant 3/4 lt. to end facing DSR in fifth position demi-plié croisé (L5).

meas. &5: Cts. &1&a2: Jeté R over turning in air 1/4 lt. to face DSL, pas de bourrée under en tournant 3/4 lt., ending croisé long fourth facing DSR.

meas. &6: Cts. &3&a4: Demi-contretemps turning 1/4 lt. to face DSL with R rond de jambe en dedans gesture (M5), landing on R; tombé forward onto L (2nd); pas de bourrée under, ending croisé long fourth.

meas. &7: Cts. &5&a6: Demi-contretemps turning 1/4 rt. to face DSR (M5) with L rond de jambe en dedans gesture, landing on L, tombé forward onto R (2nd); pas de bourrée under and L chassé forward through first, ending point tendu back croisé (L5–M5-2nd).

meas. &a8&: Cts. &a7–8&: "Catch step" by shifting weight back partially onto R and then quickly stepping forward onto L; step forward onto R, battement dégagé L forward and assemblé front (L5–M5-2nd/ H5); straighten supports in fifth position croisé (rt. to 2nd-L5).

Grand Allegro #3:

Advanced level

Music: Boston Waltz

Point tendu back croisé DSR (2nd):

intro ct. 3:	Step backward on R in demi-plié and pas de cheval L through fifth to cou-de-pied front.
meas. 1:	Relevé with développé front croisé (L5-M5-2nd).
meas. 2:	Step forward onto L (allongé) into chassé en l'air traveling forward, ending on R.
meas. &3–4:	Step forward onto L, step R forward and grand jeté croisé with R gesture attitude back croisé (L5-M5-forward diagonals with palms up).
meas. &5–6:	Coupé under, ending L cou-de-pied front (allongé 2nd); two steps forward and repeat grand jeté croisé with attitude back croisé (L5-M5-forward diagonals with palms up).
meas. &7–8:	Coupé under, ending L cou-de-pied front (allongé 2nd); two steps forward, battement dégagé L forward and assemblé croisé while traveling forward (L5-M5-2nd/H5).
meas. &9:	Petit développé R front (rt. to 2nd-L5-M5), piqué forward into 1st arabesque (L5-1st arab.).
meas. &10:	Fondu in 1st arabesque, chassé en l'air turning 1/2 lt. to face USL (2nd).
meas. &11–12:	Step forward onto L; tour jeté 1/2 lt., ending in effacé arabesque facing DSR (L5-M5-H5/rt. to 2nd), hold.
meas. 13:	Hold arabesque.
meas. &u14:	Two steps of pas de bourrée under (lt. to 2nd), step L forward on third step of pas de bourrée.
meas. &15–16:	Battement dégagé R front and glissade through fourth position stepping L through, grand jeté développé R forward (L5-M5-Cecchetti 3rd arab.), tombé L through into croisé long fourth (2nd).

Grand Allegro #4:

Intermediate level

Music: Boston Waltz

Variation I:

Point tendu front croisé DSR (2nd):

meas. 8&a: Step forward onto L with R battement dégagé front into demi-contretemps (L5-M5) in which both legs pass front [little hitchkick], landing on R; step forward on L (L5).

meas. 1: Step forward onto R and temps levé in 1st arabesque (1st arab), landing on R.

meas. 2: Step forward onto L and repeat demi-contretemps, landing on R; step L.

Repeat combination across the room beginning with meas. 1.

Variation II:

Point tendu front croisé DSR (2nd):

meas. 8&a: Step forward onto L with R battement dégagé front into demi-contretemps (L5-M5) in which both legs pass front [little hitchkick], landing on R; step forward on L (L5).

meas. 1: Step R forward and temps levé 1st arabesque (1st arab.), landing on R.

meas. 2–3: Repeat "upbeat" meas. 8&a and meas. 1.

meas. 4&a: Step L forward (L5-M5), battement dégagé R front and glissade through fourth position, landing on R.

meas. 5–6: Step L through and assemblé R over en tournant, turning 1/8 lt. to face DS (L5-2nd allongé-L5).

meas. &7: Failli turning 1/8 rt., ending croisé lunge to DSR (M5-L5).

meas. &8&a: Assemblé R over turning 1/4 lt. to DSL (2nd allongé-L5), quickly straighten L support while pivoting 1/4 rt. to face DSR (M5) and take two steps forward [R, L].

Repeat combination across room beginning with meas. 1.

Jeffery N.
Bullock

Jeffery N. Bullock

BIOGRAPHY

Jeffery Bullock began his career with the North Carolina Dance Theater following graduation from the North Carolina School of the Arts. He continued his performing career with the Pacific Northwest Ballet in Seattle and the Pittsburgh Ballet Theater. Later, he joined the contemporary dance company Hubbard Street Dance Chicago, touring the United States and Europe.

Jeffery performed in soloist and principal roles in an eclectic array of works by George Balanchine, Agnes de Mille, Alvin Ailey, Paul Taylor, Twyla Tharp, Daniel Esralow, Nacho Duato, Lucinda Childs, Glen Tetley, and others. He was also a featured performer in Paramount Pictures' *The Nutcracker* in 1986 with Pacific Northwest Ballet and was a featured performer in the 1983 PBS Special *Where Dreams Debut: The North Carolina School of the Arts.* Jeffery's work *At Midnight* earned him *Dance Magazine's* Best Choreography Nomination at the 1996 American College Dance Festival at the Kennedy Center for the Performing Arts.

He earned his MFA in choreography from the University of Iowa, was an assistant professor in the Theatre and Dance Department at the University of Texas at Austin, and is currently assistant professor at the University of Iowa.

INTERVIEW WITH JEFFERY N. BULLOCK

LC: *What is your style of teaching?*

JB: For me, the quality of movement is more important than the actual technique. I've had a lot of teachers say to me, "Jeffery, it's not classical enough. You have to do this. Don't move so much," so I had to battle for what I thought was important. I still feel that it's a good thing for dancers to move beyond the technique. So that's what I stress.

LC: *Do you think this concern about movement quality has happened because many dancers you've seen don't really move?*

JB: When I first started dancing, that was what caught my eye—dancers who moved well, whether they were modern dancers or ballet dancers. That set them apart. That's what I have tried to achieve during my career as a dancer and that's what I want to teach to other young dancers. You can have the most amazing technique, perfect turn-out, great speed, leg extension, whatever . . . but if it's boring and booklike and wooden, no one really wants to watch. To me, that's not exciting; that's not what art is. The dancer must learn to translate technique into an expression or commentary of some kind. Otherwise, why bother?

LC: *And with time, when dancers learn the movement, the technique will improve, too. Do you think the movement will assist the technique and make it stronger?*

JB: I would like to see them go hand in hand. To have one teacher who stresses movement quality and who brings out an inner quality beyond the technique, and another teacher who is more technical and teaches more of the classical technique is a great combination. I think they have to go together, and there has to be a balance.

LC: *What teachers do you feel influenced you the most?*

JB: I studied with teachers at the North Carolina School of the Arts who taught the Russian technique. But on the fringes, I had Joysanne Sidimus, who was in Balanchine's company, Mimi Paul, who was one of his principal dancers, and Robert Lindgren, who worked and studied with Balanchine. So they influenced me more with Balanchine's style than the Russian technique that I was being taught at that time.

LC: *Do you have any thoughts that you'd like to impart to students who are interested in ballet? What should they do if they're interested in joining a professional company?*

JB: They really have to do their homework. They have to go out, look at companies, and understand what the teaching, training and technique of each company is about; who is directing the company, where the director trained, who they danced with, and what will be expected of them when they audition.

LC: *Do you think going to some of the companies' summer courses is the best way to find out more about the companies?*

JB: Oh, definitely. A lot of times companies want to take dancers from their schools, even if they've only been enrolled for a year. I know that at Pacific Northwest Ballet, sometimes they'll bring young dancers there and put them in the school for a year . . .

LC: *. . . to acclimate them.*

JB: Yes, and to say a certain dancer trained at the Pacific Northwest Ballet school and now she or he is a member of the company. They want more "home-trained" dancers to join the company. It's a great way to be asked to join the company. It's an asset to know what style the company uses beforehand, especially if you're not going to the company's ballet school.

LC: *What about the ages of the women and the men? Are the men perhaps a little older when they join a company?*

JB: Yes, definitely. The average age for women getting into the companies that I've danced with, starting at the corps or apprenticeship level, is 17 or 18, sometimes 19 years old. Usually the women are very young, while the men are usually 19 or older. These are general, broad numbers based on my experience.

LC: *There is a point in time when you have to think about your future, since one cannot dance forever. Are companies doing anything to help retrain people?*

JB: There is a wonderful program in Seattle called "Beyond Dance." It's a non-profit organization that exists to support performing dancers through their career transition. It's a resource center where dancers can get information. The organization works nationally; so if you write them, they'll send you information and help you get in contact with people in the field that interests you.

LC: *I think that's fantastic.*

JB: Yes, it's a wonderful thing. Next year, I think that they're going to start offering small scholarships for dancers who are going back to school.

LC: *Do most of them go into some completely unrelated type of work, or do they stay in the arts?*

JB: Ellen Wallach [Career Transitions for Dancers in New York] did a study on that. She determined how many dancers, male and female, stayed in the field and how many moved on. I can't give you the exact numbers, but I think that more dancers stayed in the arts than went away from it. Many dancers eventually teach because that's all they know, but that is now changing. Dancers are becoming aware of the many opportunities that are out there, and I think that's important for dancers today. You have to be resourceful and explore what your own talents are, because your career as a performing dancer is going to end.

LC: *It's just like a football player. You can't do it your entire life, so you have to protect yourself and plan for the future. Hopefully, you find an area you enjoy.*

JB: Exactly. And I think that it's the responsibility of the dancer to find out what that is: Besides dancing, what else can I do? What else am I good at? Even more important, who am I?

LC: *I think the career problem is especially pervasive in ballet because dancers enter professional companies at a very young age, whereas modern dancers tend to be older and many of them have already received university degrees. The transition is not quite so difficult for them. Am I wrong?*

JB: No, you're exactly right. In ballet, you have this mentality that you must be committed to ballet and that's what you must think night and day. If anything disrupts that focus, you've lost it. Even that attitude is changing somewhat in ballet. It used to be that you did nothing else but dance—what we called the "bun-head" syndrome. But that's changing.

LC: *It's good to hear that.*

JB: Yes, because it's not working anymore for dancers. All of a sudden they find themselves 35 years old and not rehired by the company where they were employed for ten years. They're left with no job, nothing. They look back and think, I should have studied, taken classes, saved money.

LC: *Do you have any other thoughts that you'd like to express?*

JB: Yes. I think ballet especially needs to go through a reidentification of just what the art form is about. Ballet needs to totally redefine what classicism is, to be more expansive. I think it's going to have to do this, because today we're starving for new ideas. We're looking for a new way of thinking about what we're doing, especially in this country and in the smaller national companies outside of New York.

LC: *Is it difficult to find new choreographers? Most ballet dancers have probably not studied choreography and might be hesitant to choreograph.*

JB: It would be great for ballet dancers to have the opportunity to take composition classes. Maybe this could be integrated into the curriculum of ballet schools. Why shouldn't it be? I think of all the work that modern choreographers are doing today: Bill T. Jones [Cofounder and Artistic Director of Bill T. Jones/Arnie Zane Dance Company], for instance, is bringing wonderful movement and ideas to the stage.

I saw a company in Pittsburgh recently—Doug Elkins from New York. He's a choreographer who's been around for a while, but he's just now getting into the spotlight. He totally redefined for me what dance is onstage. He combined classical music, rap, jazz, classical dance, modern, hip-hop, street dance. I was stunned by what I was seeing. It was great. He deconstructed our idea of gender—women dancing together, men dancing together. Of course, I want to see more of that kind of excitement in ballet, because I think the possibilities are there.

DESCRIPTIONS

✧

Battement Tendu #1:

Advanced level

Music: Schottische #2 or #3

Fifth position croisé DSL (L5):

meas. &1:   Cts. &1&2: (M5-H5/2nd), two battement tendus front croisé with accent in.

Cts. &3&4: Pivot 1/8 rt. to face DS (lt. to 2nd) and two battement tendus front with accent in (lt. to L5 on second closing).

meas. &2:   Cts. &5&6: Pivot 1/8 rt. to face DSR (lt. through M5 to H5) and two battement tendus front effacé with accent in.

Ct. &7: Battement tendu under with accent in (lt. to 2nd on tendu out/rt. L5 on closing into fifth position croisé).

Ct. &8: Pivot 1/4 lt. to face DSL (rt. through M5 to H5) and battement tendu L under with accent in (L5/2nd on closing).

meas. &3–4:   Cts. &1–8: (lt. through M5 to H5), exact repeat of meas. 1–2 but on cts. 7–8 close R back in fifth position demi-plié croisé (lt. through 2nd to L5/rt. to L5), sous-sus (M5-H5) ending fifth position demi-plié (2nd-rt. to L5).

meas. &5–6:   Cts. &1–8: (rt. M5 to H5), repeat meas. 3–4 to other side, ending DSL.

meas. &7:   Cts. &1&2: (lt. through M5 to H5), two battement tendus back croisé with accent in.

Cts. &3&4: Pivot 1/8 rt. to face DS (lt. to 2nd) and two battement tendus back with accent in (lt. to L5 on second closing).

meas. &8&:   Cts. &5&6: Pivot 1/8 rt. to face DSR (lt. through M5 to H5) and two battement tendus back effacé with accent in.

Cts. &7&8: Battement tendu over (lt. to 2nd) with accent in, closing fifth position demi-plié (L5); sous-sus (M5-H5) ending fifth position demi-plié (2nd); straighten supports (L5).

Grand Adagio #1:

Advanced level

Music: Adagio #12

Fifth position DS with R front (L5):

meas. 1: Cts. 1–4: Développé R side (M5-2nd).

meas. 2: Cts. 5–6: Promenade 1/8 rt. to DSR into attitude front effacé (lt. to H5)

Cts. 7–8: Fondu.

meas. 3: Cts. 1–4: Straighten support and promenade 1/8 lt. to DS with gesture leg extending side (lt. to 2nd) and hold.

meas. 4: Cts. 5–8: Promenade 1/8 to DSL into attitude back effacé (rt. to H5) and hold.

meas. 5: Cts. 1–4: Promenade 3/4 lt. in attitude to DSR.

meas. 6: Cts. 5–6: Fondu croisé 2nd arabesque (croisé 2nd arab.).

Cts. &a7–8: Pas de bourrée under en tournant 3/4 rt., ending DSL in fifth position croisé sous-sus (L5-M5-H5), hold sous-sus.

meas. 7: Cts. 1–2: Remain in relevé and battement dégagé front croisé (rt. to 2nd), tombé R into croisé long fourth (2nd/M5).

Cts. 3–4: 1 1/4 pirouettes en dedans (H5), ending DSR in fifth position demi-plié croisé (2nd).

meas. 8: Ct. 5: Straighten supports (L5).

Cts. 6–8: (M5-2nd-L5).

Grand Adagio #2:

Advanced level

Music: Adagio #14

Fifth position croisé DSL (L5):

meas. 1–2:	Développé front croisé (M5-H5/2nd).
meas. 3–4:	Demi-grand rond de jambe en l'air en dehors (2nd/H5).
meas. 5–6:	Retiré side (lt. to H5) and hold.
meas. 7–8:	Promenade 1/4 rt. to DSR and développé front effacé (rt. to 2nd).
meas. 9–10:	Grand rond de jambe en l'air en dehors (2nd/L5-croisé 2nd arab.).
meas. 11–12:	(Windmill from croisé 2nd arab. to croisé 1st arab.).
meas. 13–14:	Penché arabesque.
meas. 15–16:	Come up from penché arabesque (windmill to croisé 2nd arab.).
meas. &17–18:	Step R into fourth position demi-plié croisé (2nd/M5), double pirouette en dehors (M5), ending in fourth position demi-plié croisé (croisé 2nd arab.).
meas. 19–20:	Double pirouette en dehors (H5), ending in fourth position demi-plié croisé (croisé 2nd arab.).
meas. &21–22:	Double pirouette en dehors (M5), ending croisé long fourth (croisé 2nd arab.).
meas. &23–24:	Temps lié backward (M5-allongé 2nd), close L in fifth position croisé (L5).

Grand Adagio #3:

Advanced level

Music: Adagio #12

Fifth position DS with R front (L5):

meas. 1:	Cts. 1–4: Développé R side (M5-2nd).
meas. 2:	Cts. 5–8: Promenade 3/4 rt. but change to retiré side (H5) after completing 1/4 of promenade. Continue promenade in retiré side and when reaching SL extend into 1st arabeque (1st arab.).

meas. 3–4: Ct. 1: (Allongé).

Cts. 2–5: Penché arabesque and up.

Ct. 6: Fondu arabesque.

Cts. 7–8: Pas de bourrée under [three steps in relevé] (2nd) turning 1/8 rt. to face DSL, finish in croisé sous-sus.

meas. 5–6: Ct. 1: Hold relevé and battement dégagé front croisé (lt. to H5).

Ct. 2: Tombé R into croisé lunge (lt. to 2nd).

Cts. 3–4: Bend body forward (M5).

Ct. 5: Torso returns to vertical (2nd/H5).

Cts. 6–7: Cambré back.

Ct. 8: Torso returns to vertical (rt. to 2nd).

meas. 7: Cts. 1–2: Shift weight forward, ending point tendu back croisé (M5), lower to croisé long fourth (lt. to 2nd).

Cts. 3–4: 1 1/4 pirouette en dedans (H5) to DSR, ending in fifth position demi-plié croisé (2nd).

meas. &8: Cts. &5–8: Straighten supports (allongé), bend body forward (H5 in relation to spine) and return torso to vertical (2nd-L5).

Pas de Basque and Pirouette #1:

Advanced level

Music: Lyrical Waltz #5

Fifth position croisé to DSL (L5):

meas. 1–4: Pas de basque glissé forward turning 1/4 rt. to DSR (M5-2nd-rt. to L5-croisé 2nd arab.) and close R back in fifth position croisé (L5).

meas. 5–8: Repeat meas. 1–4 to other side to end DSL.

meas. &9–10: Fondu with R petit développé front (M5), glissade forward sur les demi-pointes (2nd/H5) and hold sous-sus.

meas. &11–12: Fondu on L and pivot 1/4 rt. to face DSR with R petit développé back écarté (rt. to 2nd), glissade rt. sur les demi-pointes (allongé) and hold croisé sous-sus.

meas. &13–14: Fondu on L with R petit développé back croisé (L5-M5), glissade backward sur les demi-pointes (2nd/H5) and hold croisé sous-sus.

meas. &15–16: Demi-plié in fifth position croisé (rt. to 2nd-L5), sous-sus détourné 3/4 lt. to DSL (M5) and hold croisé sous-sus.

meas. &17–24: Demi-plié in fifth position croisé, exact repeat of meas. 1–8 [two pas de basques glissés].

meas. &25–26: Demi-plié in fifth position croisé (M5), relevé with R retiré front pivoting 1/4 rt. to DSR and hold balance (2nd/H5).

meas. 27–28: Fondu and lower R into fourth position demi-plié croisé (rt. 2nd to M5) and hold preparation.

meas. 29–30: Double pirouette en dehors (M5), ending in croisé long fourth (croisé 2nd arab.).

meas. 31–32: Shift weight forward, ending point tendu back croisé, close R back in fifth position croisé (L5).

Repeat meas. 1–32 to other side.

Pirouette #2:

Advanced level

Music: Grand Allegro Waltz

Point tendu front croisé facing DSR (2nd):

intro ct. 3: Step lt. to L fondu with R cou-de-pied front (L5).

meas. 1–2: Piqué 1st arabesque (1st arab.), fondu and chassé L forward through first (L5), ending on L in point tendu back croisé (croisé 1st arab.).

meas. &3–4: Fondu and pivot 1/4 lt. to DSL with R gesture side (2nd), continue pas de basque glissé backward, ending R point tendu front croisé (L5-M5-lt. to 2nd).

meas. &5–6: Lower R to croisé long fourth, 1 1/4 pirouettes en dedans (H5), ending DSR fondu with R cou-de-pied back (2nd).

meas. &a7–8: Pas de bourrée under en tournant 3/4 rt. to DSL, ending in fifth position demi-plié croisé (L5); chassé backward, ending point tendu front croisé (M5-2nd).

Pirouette #3:

Intermediate level

Music: Schottische #3

Fifth position croisé DSL (L5):

meas. &1:   Cts. &1–2: (M5), battement tendu front croisé (H5/2nd), lower R to croisé long fourth (2nd/M5).

Cts. 3–4: 1 1/4 pirouettes en dedans (H5) to DSR, ending in fifth position demi-plié croisé (2nd).

meas. &2:   Cts. &5–6: (rt. to L5), chassé forward, ending point tendu back croisé (croisé 2nd arab.); lower R to fourth position demi-plié croisé.

Cts. 7–8: Single pirouette en dehors (M5), ending croisé long fourth (2nd).

meas. &3:   Cts. &1–2: Petit développé R front (L5-M5), piqué 1st arabesque on R (L5-1st arab.) and tombé L through into croisé long fourth (M5).

Cts. &3–4: Repeat meas. 3 cts. &1–2.

meas. 4:   Ct. 5: (M5/2nd).

Cts. 6–8: 2 1/4 pirouettes en dedans (H5), ending DSL in fifth position demi-plié croisé (2nd).

Glissade en Tournant/Fouetté Rond de Jambe en Tournant #4:

Intermediate level

Music: Polka #1

R point tendu front en fondu facing DS (2nd/M5):

meas. &1:   Cts. &1–2: Demi-rond de jambe R side (rt. to 2nd), glissade sur les demi-pointes en tournant en dedans (M5), ending DS and releasing R leg front at end of turn (lt. to 2nd).

meas. 2:   Cts. 3–4: Fouetté rond de jambe en tournant en dehors (M5), ending DS on fondu with R dégagé front (lt. to 2nd).

meas. 3–4:   Cts. 1–4: Repeat meas. 1–2.

meas. 5–6: Cts. 1–4: Two glissades sur les demi-pointes en tournant en dedans (M5) traveling toward SR to end facing DS on fondu with R battement dégagé height front (lt. to 2nd on first turn, but on second turn both remain M5).

meas. &7: Cts. &5–6: Demi-rond de jambe R side (L5), glissade sur les demi-pointes rt. with change of legs and hold sous-sus with L front (allongé 2nd with lt. side high and rt. side low).

meas. &8: Cts. &7–8: Fondu on R with L dégagé height side (2nd), glissade sur les demi-pointes lt. with change of legs and hold sous-sus with R front (allongé 2nd with lt. side low and rt. side high).

Small Sauté #1:

Intermediate level

Music: Polka #8

Fifth position demi-plié DS with R front (L5):

meas. &1–2: Cts. &1–3: Three sautés in first position.

Ct. &4: Sauté into fifth position with L front.

meas. &3–4: Cts. &5–8: Repeat meas. 1–2 to other side, ending R front.

meas. &5–6: Cts. &1–2: Sauté into second (M5-2nd), beat R leg front and land on L with R cou-de-pied back (lt. to M5).

Cts. &3–4: Sauté into second (lt. to 2nd), beat L front and land on R with L cou-de-pied back (rt. to M5).

meas. &7–8: Ct. &5: Sauté into fourth position demi-plié with R front (M5/2nd).

Cts. 6–8: Double pirouette en dehors (M5), demi-plié in fifth position with L front (L5).

Repeat meas. 1–8 to other side.

Petit Allegro #1:

Advanced level

Music: Polka #8

Fifth position demi-plié DS with L front (2nd):

meas. &1:   Cts. &1&2: Glissade rt. without change, jeté R over (rt. to M5).

meas. &2:   Cts. &3–4: Glissade lt. without change (rt. to 2nd), jeté L over (lt. to M5).

meas. &3:   Cts. &5–6: Pivot 1/8 rt. to face DSR (rt. to M5), two steps [R, L] into grand jeté in effacé (L5-2nd arab.), landing on R.

meas. &4:   Cts. &7–8: Two steps [L, R] (M5) into grand jeté croisé (L5-croisé 2nd arab.), landing on L.

meas. &5:   Cts. &1–2: Glissade traveling backward without change (2nd), jeté R over turning 1/8 lt. to end facing DS (rt. to M5).

meas. &6:   Cts. &3–4: Glissade lt. without change (rt. to 2nd), jeté L over (lt. to M5).

meas. &7–8:   Ct. &5: Cecchetti assemblé coupé (lt. to 2nd), ending in fifth position demi-plié with L front (L5).

Cts. &6–7: Two entrechat quatre.

Ct. &8: Entrechat trois derrière, ending L cou-de-pied back (2nd/M5).

Repeat meas. 1–8 to other side.

Petit Allegro #2:

Advanced level

Music: Running Duple

Fifth position demi-plié DS with R front (demi 2nd):

meas. &1:   Cts. &1–2: Two glissades rt. with change [glissade changée].

meas. &2:   Cts. &3–4: Repeat meas. 1.

meas. &3:   Cts. &5–6: Glissade rt. without change while turning 1/8 rt. to face DSR (low M5-L5), assemblé R under (demi-second-L5).

meas. &4:   Cts. &7–8: Glissade lt. without change while turning 1/4 lt. to face DSL (low M5-L5), assemblé L under (demi-second-L5).

meas. &5:   Cts. &1–2: Glissade lt. without change while turning 1/8 rt. to face DS (low M5-L5), jeté L over (M5/2nd).

meas. &6:   Cts. &3–4: Glissade rt. without change (lt. to 2nd), jeté R over (rt. to M5).

meas. &7–8:   Cts. &5–7: Three temps levés.

             Ct. 8: Pas de bourrée under, ending in fifth position demi-plié with L front (rt. 2nd-demi-second).

Grand Allegro #1:

Advanced level

Music: Boston Waltz

Point tendu front effacé facing DSR (L5):

intro ct. 3:   (M5).

meas. &1:   Temps levé 1st arabesque on R (L5-1st arab.).

meas. 2:   Step L forward and chassé croisé en l'air traveling forward (L5-M5), landing on R.

meas. 3:   Step forward on L and temps levé with R brushing to attitude front, turning 1/4 lt. to DSL (L5-2nd-lt. to H5).

meas. 4:   Tombé into croisé long fourth (lt. to 2nd) facing DSL, then demi-contretemps turning 1/4 rt. to face DSR (M5).

meas. 5:   Temps levé 1st arabesque on R (L5-1st arab.).

meas. 6:   Step forward on L and glissade R forward through fourth (2nd).

meas. 7:   Finish glissade with L stepping through and grand jeté développé effacé (M5-Cecchetti 3rd arab.), landing on R.

meas. 8:   Step forward on L and temps levé with R cou-de-pied back (M5).

Continue repeating entire combination across floor.

Grand Allegro #2:

Advanced level

Music: Grand Allegro Waltz

Croisé to DSL with L leg in low back attitude, toe touching (2nd):

intro ct. 3: Step L to side on fondu with R cou-de-pied front (L5-M5).

meas. 1: Relevé with développé front écarté (2nd/H5).

meas. &2: Fondu and pivot 1/4 rt. to face DSR (rt. M5 then L5), temps levé in 1st arabesque on R (1st arab.).

meas. 3–4: Step L forward and pas de chat traveling toward DSR, ending L point tendu front croisé on fondu (2nd/M5).

meas. &5: Step forward onto L with R cou-de-pied back (lt. to M5), step backward onto R while brushing L back and temps levé 1st arabesque (L5-1st arab.).

meas. 6: Step L through and glissade R forward through fourth (2nd), landing on R.

meas. 7–8: Finish glissade with L stepping through and grand jeté développé effacé (Cecchetti 3rd arab.), tombé L through into croisé long fourth (2nd).

meas. &9: Rond de jambe R en dedans to front (M5), step in front of L, releasing L to cou-de-pied back; step backward onto L while brushing R back and temps levé croisé 2nd arabesque (L5-croisé 2nd arab.).

meas. 10: Chassé en l'air backward turning 1/2 rt. to face USL (2nd).

meas. 11–12: Step forward on R and tour jeté turning 1/2 rt. to end facing DSR in croisé 1st arabesque (L5-M5-H5-croisé 1st arab.).

meas. &a13: Chassé en l'air backward (2nd), step backward onto R with L cou-de-pied front (L5-M5), relevé with développé front croisé (2nd/H5).

meas. 14: Tombé L forward (rt. to 2nd), glissade R forward through fourth landing on R.

meas. 15–16: Finish glissade with L stepping through and pas de chat traveling forward turning 1/8 lt. to face DS (L5-M5-H5), ending in fifth position demi-plié with L front (2nd).

Ending Sauté #1:

Intermediate level

Music: Polka #2

Fifth position demi-plié DS with R front (L5):

meas. &1–2: Cts. &1–4: Four entrechat quatres.

meas. &3–4: Ct. &5: Sauté into second (M5-2nd).

Cts. 6–7: Shift weight to rt., relevé with L retiré side and hold (allongé with lt. side high/rt. side low).

Ct. 8: Close L front in fifth position demi-plié (L5).

Repeat meas. 1–4 to other side.

Ending Sauté #2:

Advanced level

Music: Running Duple

Croisé to DSR with R leg in low back attitude, toe touching (2nd/M5):

meas. 1: Cts. 1–2: Step brisé volé backward, ending R cou-de-pied back.

meas. 2–4: Cts. 3–8: Repeat meas. 1 three more times.

meas. &5–7: Cts. &1–6: Brush R forward, six brisés over.

meas. &8: Cts. &7–8: Glissade rt. without change while turning 1/8 lt. to face DS (rt. to 2nd), jeté R over turning 1/8 lt. to face DSL (lt. to M5).

Ending Sauté #3:

Intermediate level

Music: Polka #2

Fifth position demi-plié DS with R front (L5):

meas. &1–2: Cts. &1–4: Four entrechat quatres.

meas. &3–4:   Cts. &5–7: Pivot 1/8 rt. to DSR as R chassés backward through first (M5), relevé in attitude back croisé (2nd/H5) and hold.

Ct. &8: Pivot 1/8 lt. to face DS and demi-plié in fifth position with R closing back (rt. to 2nd-L5).

Repeat meas. 1–4 to other side.

Ending Tours #1 (Women):

Advanced level

Music: Coda

Point tendu front croisé to DSL (2nd/M5):

meas. &1–2:   Cts. &1–4: Fondu and demi-rond de jambe R (rt. to 2nd), piqué turn en dedans (M5) and coupé L under (lt. to 2nd). Repeat piqué turn en dedans.

meas. &3–4:   Cts. &5–8: Demi-rond de jambe (rt. to 2nd), piqué emboîté en tournant by half turns (M5) [1/2 piqué turn to rt. with L retiré front, 1/2 piqué turn rt. with R retiré front to face DSL and repeat for a total of two full revolutions], quickly coupé L under with R dégagé height front croisé (lt. to 2nd).

meas. &5–6:   Cts. &1–4: Demi-rond de jambe (rt. to 2nd), two piqué turns en dedans (M5).

meas. &7–8:   Cts. &5–7: Demi-rond de jambe (rt. to 2nd), chaînés (M5) toward DSR with 3/4 turn on last step [L] in order to face DSR.

Ct. 8: Fondu on L and chassé R through fifth position and forward, ending point tendu back effacé (H5/2nd).

Ending Tours #2 (Men):

Advanced level

Music: March #2

Point tendu front écarté to DSL (2nd/M5):

meas. 1:   Cts. 1–4: Step R side and two saut de basques turning rt. (M5).

meas. 2:   Cts. 5–8: Four emboîtés en tournant turning rt. [two complete revolutions].

meas. 3:   Cts. 1–4: Two saut de basques turning rt. (M5).

meas. &4:   Cts. &5–6: Pivot 1/8 rt. to face DS, chassé R forward (2nd), step L behind with R battement dégagé front and assemblé front, ending fifth position demi-plié with R front (rt. to M5).

Cts. 7–8: Double tour en l'air (lt. to M5) rt., ending fifth position demi-plié with L front.

Margaret McLaughlin
Blair

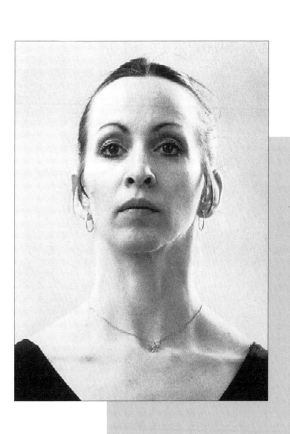

Margaret McLaughlin Blair

BIOGRAPHY

Margaret McLaughlin Blair's professional career in dance began in 1962, when she was an apprentice/scholarship student at the Joffrey Ballet. She was privileged to study directly under Robert Joffrey, as well as with Gerald Arpino and Hector Zaraspe, among others.

Her dancing career includes the San Francisco Ballet (1972–1974) under Lew Christiansen and Michael Smuin; the Milwaukee Ballet (1974–1978), where, in addition to dancing soloist and principal roles, she served as ballet mistress and master teacher; and the Hamburg Ballet (1978–1984) under John Neumeier. While in Hamburg, Margaret danced soloist and principal roles by John Neumeier and Murray Louis, and worked with world-class artists Galina Ulanova, Anton Dolin, Irina Jacobson and Marcia Haydée, among others. The Hamburg Ballet toured internationally, playing cities such as Rio de Janiero, Leningrad, Dresden, Paris, Buenos Aires, Berlin and New York.

Margaret has been teaching classical ballet since 1971, when she taught classes for the Connecticut Ballet School. Since retiring in 1984 from her dancing career, she has had a busy and demanding schedule as dance teacher and private coach. In addition to her position as principal teacher with the Milwaukee Ballet school, she guest teaches at dance schools and universities throughout the nation and coaches both students and professional dancers.

In the early '90s, Margaret joined the Ballet du Nord, teaching in the school and serving briefly as ballet mistress. She is presently ballet mistress at Les Ballets de Monte Carlo.

INTERVIEW WITH MARGARET McLAUGHLIN BLAIR

ᘓ

LC: *Which teachers do you feel influenced you the most?*

MB: My very first teacher, when I was very young, was an amazing woman. She was also Merrill Ashley's [NYCB principal dancer] first teacher—Phyllis Marmein. She was originally with the Vic-Wells Ballet. She was one of those extraordinary people who gave you a great love for dance, a great feeling for dance. When I was about 11 years old she said to my parents, "I've taken Margaret as far as I can; she has to go somewhere else." Extraordinary woman.

LC: *Very honest!*

MB: Yes. She's still alive, 82 years old. She went down to New York City (from Schenectady) and checked out all the schools for me and decided on the Joffrey; I was transferred directly into the hands of Robert Joffrey himself. He was still teaching every evening class when I studied there. So the second influence—probably the most important one—was Mr. Joffrey. I trained in his school until I was 18 or so, as a scholarship student and an apprentice. I left, but throughout my career, Mr. Joffrey was always there. He saw me dance and he was always supportive. No matter what I did, even up to the last time I saw him, he was encouraging, still being positive about my work, still interested. In fact, at one point I quit dancing for a short period. Mr. Joffrey found out and said to me, "Margaret, what are you doing? You must go back to dance. It's very important for you."

LC: *It's amazing with all the people and students he knew that he was able to keep tabs on you.*

MB: Unbelievable. He would say things on purpose in front of my directors. He knew how important it was. He did it with two different directors; the last one was John Neumeier, backstage at the Brooklyn Academy of Music (John had brought the Hamburg Ballet to New York). Mr. Joffrey and I were talking, when John came up and said, "Margaret, you *know* Mr. Joffrey?" Mr. Joffrey put his arm around me and said, "Oh yes. Margaret was one of my baby ballerinas." He *knew* how that would change my image in John's eyes.

My last teacher was Truman Finney, who was ballet master in Hamburg.

Technically I am still very influenced by him. He was absolutely right in his approach to technique, in terms of placement, rotation of the thighs, use of the feet and coordination of the upper body. He used to make me so angry! We'd do one of John Neumeier's four-hour modern ballets and the next morning at ten a.m. we'd have a killer classical ballet class. You just wanted to wring Truman's neck! But he was right.

LC: *Are there any other teachers who have influenced you?*

MB: Yes, Maggie Black. Not so much from a technical standpoint as from motivation and her very positive approach to dance. I had wonderful teachers at Joffrey: Hector Zaraspe and Perry Brunson especially. They tended to be what we would call "old school" and used to scare the living daylights out of me. I find that, as much as I loved them and what they did for me, I can't teach like that. I need to reach the dancer from a positive standpoint, like Mr. Joffrey, Phyllis Marmein and Maggie did.

LC: *People just work well in varying circumstances; some work well with a real disciplinarian, which scares others—they need more of a nurturing teacher.*

MB: Yes. Absolutely. As far as discipline, though, I'm quite tough with the little ones. The younger the kids, the tougher I am. Then, as they get older, I get easier.

LC: *Do you feel that you stress one thing beyond all others in your teaching?*

MB: I try not to! I've always heard that most people stress the thing they were strongest in as a dancer, and I find myself doing the opposite. I moved well, had the strange, elusive thing known as "quality" and was lucky enough to have a sense of musicality—"technique be damned." As a teacher, I stress technique, maybe even too much. I want to get at it in all ways, from movement and from dramatics. I was very much a dramatic dancer, constantly fighting with my technique; and as a teacher, I'm doing just the opposite—constantly screaming technique. It's funny, because it's not what I'm really interested in; I'm interested in what one *does* with the technique.

LC: *Were you trained in one specific method?*

MB: No. I don't think so.

LC: *Eclectic?*

MB: Yes, the Joffrey school was very clean—clean technique, clean upper body. I'm told that people can still recognize me as a Joffrey-trained dancer because of the very clean lines. I don't know exactly where Mr. Joffrey got that except from his own good taste. He took the best from everything he had learned. I have added more to that, but I keep coming back to my Joffrey training. I'm also fascinated with what the Kirov does. I have no training in that method, but since Truman Finney in Hamburg was very involved in Kirov training, there probably is an influence through him.

LC: *Would you have any wise words for young people who are interested in dancing professionally? Or do you think that some of them should not set their sights quite so high, since there's so much competition now?*

MB: It's *always* been hard. I used to think that if you really love something, and really want it, you can achieve it. But in my second year in San Francisco I realized that there were several ballet companies folding. I counted the actual number of AGMA jobs there were, and there were only 500 and I had one of them. I felt extremely lucky. Now there are so many levels at which you can dance: the civic level, regional companies, professional companies. . . . I was certainly lucky to land in Hamburg, which now has one of the great companies in Europe—actually in the world.

LC: *Do you think some young dancers should try to prepare themselves for other kinds of employment as well as dancing?*

MB: I have a real problem there. We counsel our students, "Keep your options open. Think about going to college. Think about other aspects of dance careers: arts administration," and we tell them to keep involved in other things. And, yet, I realize that the way I made it as a professional dancer was to do *nothing* else but dance. By the time I was 12 years old, I was taking three classes a day. Maybe that's what it takes to become a professional.

LC: *I think also that knowing the right people, or being in the right place at the right time, has a great deal to do with success.*

MB: Oh, absolutely. I know that my training at Joffrey probably made all the difference in the world. The training I got, the people I met, Mr. Joffrey's support throughout my career were some of the things that made my life in dance work. Of course, then you may face the situation that at 34 or 35 years old you have to quit dancing and you have no options left. I did a lot of teaching as ballet mistress in Milwaukee while I was dancing. It used to drive me crazy. Slowly I got into it after retiring and discovered I really liked it. When you retire, you can go back to school, but a lot of us can't afford it; we have no money. I'm really concerned about what to tell young students. On the one hand, if they want a professional life in dance, I don't know if we should be telling them to explore other avenues, because the amount of time that needs to be spent in the studio has to be spent there, but by the same token you narrow yourself that way.

LC: *As an adviser of university students, I stress that they try to find a second-ary area that is of importance to them, because teaching jobs are scarce. If they graduate and cannot find a company to perform with or a teaching job, they have to have options.*

MB: Right. I just happened to luck out in liking teaching so much and finding employment. But not everybody likes teaching, and not everybody is good at it.

LC: *I think many people don't have the patience.*

MB: Just because you're a good professional dancer doesn't mean you'll be a good teacher. And, as you say, teaching jobs are few and far between. I finally real-ized the other day that Taras Kalba and I are the only two salaried, principal teach-ers with the Milwaukee Ballet school. Therefore, I have one of two jobs at that level in the entire state of Wisconsin, because that's the only professional school attached to a professional company in the state. There are only *two* jobs like that!

LC: *Is there anything else you wish to add?*

MB: Yes. As a teacher I'm learning constantly.

DESCRIPTIONS

✾

Battement Tendu #1:

Intermediate level

Music: Gavotte #2

Fifth position croisé DSL (M5/2nd):

meas. 1: Cts. 1–2: Battement tendu front croisé and close in fifth position croisé.

Cts. 3–4: Repeat cts. 1–2.

meas. 2: Cts. 5–6: Battement dégagé front croisé, fondu with R cou-de-pied front (rt. to M5).

Cts. 7–8: Straighten support and point tendu front croisé (H5/2nd), close R in fifth position croisé (lt. to 2nd-L5).

meas. 3: Cts. 1–2: Battement tendu back croisé (2nd/M5) and close in fifth position croisé.

Cts. 3–4: Repeat cts. 1–2 of meas. 3.

meas. 4: Cts. 5–6: Battement dégagé back croisé, fondu with L cou-de-pied back (lt. to M5).

Cts. 7–8: Straighten support and point tendu back croisé (2nd/H5), close L in fifth position croisé (rt. to 2nd-L5).

meas. 5: Cts. 1–2: Pivot 1/8 rt. to face DS with R battement tendu side (M5-2nd), close R back in fifth position.

Cts. 3–4: Battement tendu R side and close R front in fifth position.

meas. 6: Cts. 5–6: Battement dégagé R side, fondu with R cou-de-pied back (M5).

Cts. 7–8: Straighten support and point tendu R side (2nd), close R front in fifth position.

meas. &7: Cts. &1–2: Quickly demi-plié in fifth position (rt. to L5), relevé with R retiré front (rt. to M5), demi-plié in fifth position with R front.

Cts. 3–4: Repeat cts. 1–2 of meas. 7.

meas. 8: Cts. 5–7: Relevé and pivot 1/8 rt. to face DSR with R retiré front and balance (lt. to M5).

Ct. 8: Demi-plié in fifth position croisé (L5).

Grand Battement #1:

Intermediate level

Music: March #2

Fifth position DS with R front (2nd):

meas. 1: Cts. 1–2: Grand battement R side and close back in fifth position.

Cts. 3–4: Grand battement L side and close back in fifth position.

meas. &2: Cts. &5–6: Quickly raise R retiré front (L5-M5), développé R side (H5) and hold extension.

Cts. &7–8: Quickly close R back in fifth position, développé L side and hold extension.

meas. &3: Cts. &1–2: Close L back in fifth position (2nd), grand battement L side and close front in fifth position.

Cts. 3–4: Grand battement R side and close front in fifth position.

meas. &4&: Cts. &5–6: Quickly raise L retiré back (L5-M5), développé L side (H5) and hold extension.

Cts. &7–8&: Quickly close L front in fifth position, développé R side and hold extension, close R front in fifth position.

Battement Fondu with Relevé #1:

Advanced level

Music: Gavotte #2

Fifth position croisé DSL (M5/2nd):

meas. 1: Cts. 1–2: Battement fondu with R cou-de-pied front, straighten support and point front croisé.

meas. 2&:   Cts. 3–4&: Battement fondu with R cou-de-pied front, relevé and grand battement front croisé (lt. to H5), quickly close R front in sous-sus.

meas. 3:   Cts. 5–6: Battement fondu with L cou-de-pied back (2nd/M5), straighten support and point back croisé.

meas. 4&:   Cts. 7–8&: Battement fondu with L cou-de-pied back, relevé and grand battement back croisé (rt. to H5), quickly close L back in sous-sus.

meas. 5:   Cts. 1–2: Pivot 1/8 rt. to face DS on fondu with R cou-de-pied front (rt. to 2nd), relevé with R side at dégagé height.

meas. 6:   Cts. 3–4: Step R to side on fondu and pivot 1/2 rt. to face US with L cou-de-pied back, relevé with L side at dégagé height.

meas. 7:   Cts. 5–6: Step L to side on fondu and pivot 1/2 rt. to face DS with R cou-de-pied front, relevé with R side at dégagé height.

meas. 8:   Cts. 7–8: Hold relevé, pivot 1/8 rt. to face DSR, closing R leg back in fifth position croisé (L5).

Grand Adagio #1:

Advanced level

Music: Adagio #13

In this example, two counts are the equivalent of one measure of 6/8.

Fifth position croisé DSL (L5):

meas. 1:   Cts. 1–2: R retiré front (M5), développé front croisé on fondu.

meas. 2&:   Cts. 3–4&: Straighten L support and demi-grand rond de jambe en l'air en dehors while pivoting 1/4 rt. to face DSR (2nd/H5), single rond de jambe en l'air en dehors, close R back in fifth position croisé (rt. to 2nd-L5).

meas. 3–4&:   Cts. 5–8&: Repeat meas. 1–2 to other side and end croisé facing DSL, close L back in fifth position croisé.

meas. 5:   Cts. 1–2: Repeat cts. 1–2 in meas. 1.

meas. 6–7:   Ct. 3–4&a: Straighten L support and begin demi-grand rond de jambe en l'air en dehors while pivoting 1/4 rt. to face DSR (2nd/H5). Continue grand rond de jambe en l'air, ending attitude back croisé on fondu (lt. through L5 to H5/rt. to 2nd) with torso folded over lt. [renversé] and pas de bourrée piqué under (lt. to 2nd) en tournant 3/4 to rt.

Ct. 5: Finish pas de bourrée in croisé long fourth facing DSL (rt. to M5).

Ct. 6: 1 3/8 pirouettes en dedans in attitude back (H5/2nd).

meas. 8:   Cts. 7&a8: Complete pirouette, ending fondu in 1st arabesque (1st arab.) facing SR, quickly pas de bourrée under turning 1/8 lt. to end facing DSR in fifth position croisé (2nd-L5).

Grand Adagio #2:

Advanced level

Music: Adagio #10

Fifth position croisé DSL (L5):

meas. 1–2:   Torso folds to rt. (rt. to 2nd) and returns to vertical, then folds to left (rt. to H5 in relation to spine).

meas. 3–4:   Torso folds to front (rt. to M5) and returns to vertical (rt. through 2nd-L5).

meas. 5–8:   Repeat port de bras to other side with lt. arm.

meas. &9–10:   (M5), battement tendu front croisé (2nd), fondu and port de bras forward over extended leg (H5 in relation to spine).

meas. 11–12:   Straighten support and lift leg front to battement height as torso returns to vertical (arms remain H5 in relation to spine).

meas. 13–14:   Promenade 1/4 rt. to DSR with demi-grand rond de jambe en l'air en dehors.

meas. 15–16:   Continue grand rond de jambe en l'air, ending attitude back croisé on fondu (rt. to 2nd) and fold torso lt. [renversé].

meas. 17–18:   Pas de bourrée piqué under en tournant (lt. to 2nd) turning 7/8 rt. to end DS in fifth position demi-plié with R front (L5).

meas. 19–20:   Straighten supports and développé R side (M5-H5).

meas. 21–24:   Fouetté pivoting 1/4 lt. to end facing SL in 1st arabesque (1st arab.).

meas. 25–28:   Penché arabesque and up.

meas. &29–30: Rise and pivot 1/8 rt. to face DSL, tombé R through with L cou-de-pied back (windmill from 1st arab. to croisé 1st arab.) and pas de bourrée under en tournant 3/4 lt. (2nd) to end facing DSR in fifth position demi-plié croisé (L5).

meas. &31–32: Petit développé L front (M5), piqué forward into croisé 2nd arabesque and hold (L5-croisé 2nd arab.), demi-plié fifth position croisé (L5).

Grand Adagio #3:

Intermediate level

Music: Adagio #12

Fifth position croisé DSL (2nd):

meas. 1: Cts. 1–2: Grand plié (rt. to M5).

Cts. 3–4: Relevé from grand plié with R retiré front while pivoting 1/4 rt. to face DSR (H5), lower on straight support into attitude back croisé (lt. to 2nd).

meas. 2: Cts. 5–7: Hold position.

Ct. 8: Close R back in fifth position croisé (rt. to 2nd).

meas. 3–4: Cts. 1–8: Repeat meas. 1–2 to other side to end facing DSL (lt. to 2nd-L5).

meas. 5: Cts. 1–4: Pivot 1/8 rt. to face DS and développé R side (M5-2nd/H5).

meas. &6: Ct. &5: Single rond de jambe en l'air en dehors.

Ct. 6: Fouetté 1/4 lt. to face SL in 1st arabesque (1st arab.).

Cts. 7–8: Promenade 5/8 lt. in 1st arabesque to end facing DSR.

meas. 7: Cts. 1–3: Change gesture to attitude back (2nd/H5) and continue promenade one full revolution lt., ending DSR.

Ct. 4: Fondu and lower R to croisé long fourth (M5/2nd).

meas. 8: Ct. 5: 1 1/4 pirouettes en dedans (M5).

Cts. 6&7: End DSL in fifth position demi-plié croisé, glissade rt. with change while turning 1/4 rt. (2nd), ending DSR in fifth demi-plié croisé (L5).

Ct. 8: Straighten supports (M5-2nd).

Grand Adagio #4:

Intermediate level

Music: Adagio #13a

In this example, two counts are the equivalent of one measure of 6/8.

Fifth position croisé DSL (2nd):

intro ct. 8:   Ct. 8: Battement tendu front croisé (L5-M5-2nd).

meas. 1:   Cts. 1–2: Fondu and port de bras forward over extended leg (H5 in relation to spine).

meas. 2:   Cts. 3–4: Straighten support and lift leg front to battement height as torso returns to vertical (arms remain H5 in relation to spine).

meas. 3:   Cts. 5–6: R retiré side and hold.

meas. 4:   Cts. 7–8: Pass leg to attitude back effacé and hold (lt. to 2nd).

meas. 5:   Cts. 1–2: Pivot 1/4 rt. to face DSR with R retiré side (M5).

meas. 6:   Cts. 3–4: Développé to front effacé (H5/2nd).

meas. &7:   Cts. 5&a–6: Brush R through first (lt. begins to move to lt. back diagonal/rt. to L5), fondu in croisé 2nd arabesque (finish in croisé 2nd arab.), pas de bourrée piqué under (2nd) en tournant 3/4 rt. to end in croisé long fourth facing DSL (rt. to M5).

meas. 8:   Cts. 7–8: 1 1/4 pirouettes en dedans (H5), ending DSR in fifth position demi-plié croisé (M5-2nd).

Pirouette #1:

Advanced level

Music: Mazurka #2

Face DS in low back attitude, R toe touching (hands on waist):

meas. 1:   Cts. 1–3: Step R side (2nd) and temps levé with L cou-de-pied back, torso folding lt. (L5/rt. side high with focus to lt. side low).

meas. 2&:   Cts. 4–6&: Repeat meas. 1 to other side (2nd-lt. side high/L5), pivot 1/8 rt. to face DSR (2nd/M5).

meas. 3:   Cts. 1–3: Step forward onto R in fondu arabesque (rt. to H5), arabesque sautillée [two "chugs"].

meas. &4: Cts. &4–6: Deepen fondu and rond de jambe L gesture to lt. (rt. to 2nd), one "step-over" turn [piqué tourné en dehors] (M5), ending DSR battement dégagé front effacé en fondu (H5/2nd).

meas. 5–6: Ct. 1: Tombé forward onto R (lt. to 2nd).

Cts. 2–4: Pas de bourrée under, ending fourth position demi-plié croisé (rt. through L5 to M5).

Cts. 5–6: Maintain pirouette preparation.

meas. 7: Cts. 1–3: Triple pirouette en dehors (M5).

meas. 8: Cts. 4–6: End pirouette DSR croisé long fourth (croisé 2nd arab.), shift weight forward, ending point tendu back croisé; close R back in fifth position croisé (hands on waist).

Pirouette #2:

Advanced level

Music: Big Waltz #1

Fifth position croisé DSL (2nd):

intro ct. 3: Battement dégagé R side.

meas. 1–2: Balancé rt. and fold torso over lt. side (lt. side low/rt. side high), balancé left and fold torso over rt. side (lt. side high/rt. through L5 crossing body to lt. side low).

meas. &3–4: Pivot 1/4 rt. to face DSR (M5), tombé forward onto R (2nd) and pas de bourrée under, ending in fourth position demi-plié croisé (L5).

meas. &5–6: Petit développé R front effacé (M5); piqué 1st arabesque and hold (1st arab.); tombé L through, ending fourth position demi-plié croisé (2nd/M5).

meas. 7–8: Single pirouette en dehors (M5), ending fourth position demi-plié croisé (lt. to 2nd).

meas. 9–10: Double pirouette en dehors (M5), ending fourth position demi-plié croisé (lt. to 2nd).

meas. 11–12: Double pirouette en dehors (M5), ending on relevé with R dégagé front effacé (H5/2nd).

meas. &13–14: Tombé forward on R (2nd/M5), three chaîné turns rt. beginning with L support [three full revolutions with sixth step on R tombé facing DSR] (M5).

meas. 15–16: "Step-over" turn [piqué tourné en dehors] on L, ending DSR in fifth position demi-plié croisé (2nd).

Pirouette #3:

Advanced level

Music: Big Waltz #2

Point tendu front croisé facing DSR (2nd):

intro ct. 3: Step L forward (lt. begins sweep forward through L5).

meas. 1–2: Little leap forward onto R to begin 1/2 waltz (lt. sweeps forward/ rt. back diagonal low), 1/2 balancé turn (2nd-L5-M5) to end facing DSR.

meas. 3–4: Tombé forward onto R (2nd), pas de bourrée under, ending in fourth position demi-plié croisé and hold (rt. through L5 to M5).

meas. 5–6: Double pirouette en dehors (M5), ending in croisé long fourth (croisé 2nd arab.).

meas. 7: Détourné 3/4 rt. to end facing DSL with R point tendu front croisé (M5-H5/2nd).

meas. 8: Hold position.

meas. &9–16: Step forward onto R (rt. begins sweep forward through L5), repeat meas. 1–8 to other side.

meas. 17–20: Exact repeat of meas. 1–3, but end DSR in croisé long fourth (M5/2nd).

meas. 21–22: 1 1/4 pirouettes en dedans (M5), ending DSL in fifth position demi-plié croisé.

meas. &23–24: Quickly deepen demi-plié (L5), sous-sus and détourné (2nd-H5) 3/4 lt. to face DSR and hold croisé sous-sus, demi-plié in fifth position croisé (2nd).

meas. 25–32: Straighten R support and pivot 1/4 lt. to face DSL with L battement dégagé front effacé (rt. begins sweep forward through L5), repeat meas. 17–24 to other side, but end by straightening supports in fifth position.

Pirouette #4:

Advanced level

Music: Big Waltz #2

Fifth position croisé DSL (L5):

intro ct. 3: (M5).

meas. 1–2: Battement tendu front croisé (H5/2nd) and lower R into croisé long fourth (2nd/rt. L5 to M5).

meas. 3–4: 1 1/4 pirouettes en dedans in attitude back to DSR (H5/2nd), at end of turn while still on relevé, open L in arabesque and hold (allongé 2nd position with lt. side high); tombé L through (2nd).

meas. &5–6: Pivot on L 1/4 lt. to face DSL, step onto R to rt. side and balancé turning 3/4 lt. (lt. moves slowly to M5/rt. through H5 to M5), ending DSR in fourth position demi-plié croisé (lt. to 2nd).

meas. 7–8: Single pirouette en dehors (M5), ending in fourth position demi-plié croisé (lt. to 2nd) and hold demi-plié.

meas. 9–10: Double pirouette en dehors (M5), ending in fourth position demi-plié croisé (lt. to 2nd) and hold demi-plié.

meas. 11–12: Triple pirouette en dehors (M5), ending in fourth position demi-plié croisé (lt. to 2nd), quickly relevé on L and détourné one full turn rt. with R front at dégagé height (M5-lt. 2nd at end of turn); tombé forward onto R with L dégagé side (rt. to 2nd).

meas. 13: Single "step-over" turn (M5) [piqué tourné en dehors] and tombé forward onto R (2nd).

meas. 14–16: Single "step-over" turn (M5) with R tombé forward (2nd) followed by double "step-over" turn (M5) to end facing DSR in fifth position demi-plié croisé (2nd).

Pirouette #5:

Advanced level

Music: Big Waltz #3

Point tendu back croisé facing DSL (2nd):

meas. 8&a: Pas de bourrée over en tournant turning rt. to end facing DSL with R battement dégagé height front croisé (L5-M5).

meas. 1–4:   Renversé en dehors with relevé on L (H5) turning 1/4 rt. to face DSR as R executes grand rond de jambe en l'air en dehors, ending fondu in attitude back croisé (rt. to 2nd); pas de bourrée piqué under en tournant (lt. to 2nd-M5) turning 3/4 rt. to end facing DSL on fondu with R point tendu front croisé (Cecchetti 3rd arab.).

meas. &5–7:   Demi-rond de jambe R side at dégagé height (2nd), two single piqué turns en dedans (M5) followed by double piqué turn en dedans to end facing DSL (2nd/M5) on fondu with R battement dégagé height front.

meas. 8:   Tombé forward onto R with L cou-de-pied back, step L behind R and pivot 1/4 rt. to face DSR with R front at dégagé height (lt. begins sweep through L5/rt. to 2nd).

meas. 9–10:   Little leap forward onto R and execute 1/2 waltz turn (lt. sweeps forward into arab./rt. moves to back diagonal low-2nd), 1/2 balancé turn (L5-M5) to end facing DSR with R battement dégagé height front effacé.

meas. 11–12:   Tombé forward onto R (2nd) and pas de bourrée under, ending in fourth position demi-plié croisé (rt. through L5 to M5), hold demi-plié.

meas. 13–14:   Double pirouette en dehors (M5), ending in fourth position demi-plié croisé (lt. to 2nd), hold demi-plié.

meas. 15–16:   Double pirouette en dehors (M5), ending in croisé long fourth (2nd).

Pirouette #6:

Intermediate level

Music: Mazurka #1

Face DSR in low back attitude, R toe touching (lt. hand on waist/2nd):

meas. 1:   Cts. 1–3: Mazurka step on R (rt. to M5).

meas. 2:   Cts. 4–6: Mazurka step on L (rt. to 2nd).

meas. 3–4:   Cts. 1–6: Tombé forward on R and pas de bourrée under, ending in fourth position demi-plié croisé (rt. through L5 to M5).

meas. 5–6:   Cts. 1–6: Triple pirouette en dehors (rt. to M5), ending in fourth demi-plié croisé.

meas. 7:   Cts. 1–3: Double pirouette en dehors (rt. 2nd to H5), ending in croisé long fourth.

meas. 8:   Ct. 4: Remain in croisé long fourth and fold torso over lt. (rt. allongé side high).

Ct. 5&: Hold position on ct. 5, shift weight forward, ending point tendu back croisé with torso coming to vertical (rt. to 2nd) on "&."

Ct. 6: Close R back in fifth position croisé.

Petit Allegro #1:

Advanced level

Music: Allegro 6/8

In this example, two counts are the equivalent of one measure of 6/8.

Fifth position demi-plié croisé DSL (L5):

meas. &1:   Cts. &1&2: Sissonne fermée moving forward (croisé 2nd arab.), sissonne fermée moving backward (M5/2nd).

meas. &2:   Cts. &3&4: Sissonne fermée L over turning 1/8 rt. to face DS, sissonne fermée R over (2nd/M5).

meas. &3:   Cts. &5&a6: Straighten L support and dégagé R side (rt. to 2nd), tombé to rt. side, pas de bourrée under, ending fifth position demi-plié with L front (rt. to M5).

meas. &4:   Cts. &7&8: Battement dégagé R side, two brisés over.

meas. &5–8:   Cts. &1–8: Repeat meas. 1–4 on other side with first sissonne fermée traveling forward turning 1/8 to rt. to face DSR (croisé 2nd arab.).

meas. &9–11:   Cts. &1–6: Exact repeat of meas. 1–3. First sissonne fermée traveling forward makes 1/8 turn to lt. to face DSL (croisé 2nd arab.).

meas. &12:   Cts. &7&a8: Jeté R over (2nd-L5/H5) with torso folding over lt. side, pas de bourrée under turning 7/8 lt. with torso coming to vertical during turn (rt. through M5 to L5), finish facing DSR in fifth position demi-plié croisé.

meas. &13–16:   Cts. &1–8: Repeat meas. 9–12 on other side, ending combination in fifth position demi-plié croisé facing DSL.

Petit Allegro #2:

Advanced level

Music: Polka #3

Fifth position demi-plié croisé DSL (L5):

meas. &1:	Cts. &1&2: Turning 1/4 rt. in air to face DSR, ballotté forward (M5-rt. to 2nd) and ballotté backward (2nd/M5).
meas. 2:	Cts. 3&4: Step L behind R (rt. to 2nd) and ballonné R under (L5) turning 1/8 lt. to face DS.
meas. &3:	Cts. &5&a6: Straighten L support and battement dégagé R side (M5), tombé to rt. side (2nd) and pas de bourrée under, ending in fifth position demi-plié with L front.
meas. &4:	Cts. &7&8: Jeté R over (rt. to M5), step L behind R (rt. to 2nd) and assemblé R under (L5).
meas. &5–8:	Cts. &1–8: Repeat meas. &1–4 on other side with first ballotté turning 1/8 lt. in air to face DSL. Meas. 8 ends DS with R front in fifth position demi-plié.
meas. &9–10:	Cts. &1–4: Exact repeat of meas. 1–2 with first ballotté turning 1/8 rt. in air to face DSR.
meas. &11&:	Cts. &5–6&: Jeté traveling to rt. side (2nd), ending with L cou-de-pied front (L5), jeté traveling forward with R attitude back (M5-forward diagonals with palms up).
meas. &12:	Cts. &7&8: Cecchetti assemblé coupé (L5) and entrechat quatre.
meas. &13–16:	Cts. &1–8: Repeat meas. &9–12 on other side. First ballotté turns 1/8 lt. in air to face DSL. Meas. 16 ends DS with R front in fifth position demi-plié.

Petit Allegro #3:

Advanced level

Music: Running Duple

Fifth position demi-plié DS with L front (2nd):

meas. &1:	Cts. &1&2: Glissade rt. without change, jeté R over (rt. to M5).
meas. &2:	Cts. &3&4: Repeat cts. 1–2 to other side (rt. to 2nd-lt. to M5).

meas. &3:   Cts. &5&6: Exact repeat of cts. 1–2 (lt. to 2nd-rt. to M5).

meas. 4:   Cts. 7&8: Step L behind R (rt. to 2nd) and ballonné R under (L5) turning 1/8 rt. to face DSR.

meas. 5:   Cts. 1&2: Step R behind L (2nd/M5) and ballonné L front, ending L cou-de-pied front.

meas. &6:   Cts. &3&4: Ballonné L under (rt. opens 2nd-L5) turning 1/8 lt. to face DS, dégagé L back and assemblé (croisé 2nd arab.-L5) turning 1/8 lt. to face DSL, ending in fifth position demi-plié croisé.

meas. &7:   Cts. &5&6: Entrechat trois derrière [R ends cou-de-pied back] turning 1/4 rt. to face DSR, assemblé back (croisé 2nd arab.-L5), ending in fifth position demi-plié croisé.

meas. &8:   Cts. &7&8: Entrechat trois derrière [L ends cou-de-pied back] turning 1/4 lt. to face DSL, assemblé back (L5-croisé 2nd arab.), ending in fifth position demi-plié croisé.

Petit Allegro #4:

Advanced level

Music: Running Duple

Fifth position demi-plié DS with L front (2nd):

meas. &1:   Cts. &1&2: Glissade rt. without change, jeté R over (rt. to M5).

meas. &2:   Cts. &3&4: Repeat cts. 1–2 to other side (rt. to 2nd-lt. to M5).

meas. 3:   Cts. 5&6: Pivot 1/8 rt. to face DSR as R steps behind L (2nd/M5), cabriole front croisé traveling toward DSR.

meas. &4:   Cts. &7&8: Two more cabrioles front traveling toward DSR.

meas. 5:   Cts. 1&2: Leap forward onto L (croisé 2nd arab.), cabriole back traveling toward USL.

meas. &6:   Cts. &3&4: One more cabriole back, Cecchetti assemblé coupé (L5), ending in fifth position demi-plié croisé.

meas. &7:   Cts. &5&a6: Entrechat trois derrière [L ends cou-de-pied back] turning 1/8 lt. to face DS (M5-lt. to 2nd), pas de bourrée under, ending in fifth position demi-plié with L front (rt. to 2nd-L5).

meas. &8:   Cts. &7&a8: Entrechat cinq derrière [R ends cou-de-pied back] (M5-rt. to 2nd), pas de bourrée under, ending in fifth position demi-plié with R front (lt. to 2nd-L5).

Petit Allegro #5:

Advanced level

Music: Polka #3

Point tendu front croisé DSR (2nd):

intro ct. 8:   Ct. 8: Step forward onto L (lt. to M5).

meas. &1–2:   Cts. &1–4: Battement dégagé R front, four ballonnés front traveling toward DSR.

meas. &3–4:   Cts. &5–8: Four big emboîtés [gesture in low attitude front] (on first emboîté lt. to 2nd) traveling toward DSR.

meas. 5:   Cts. 1–2: Step R forward and saut de basque (M5) traveling toward DSR.

meas. 6:   Cts. 3–4: Repeat step saut de basque.

meas. &7:   Cts. 5&a6: Extend R front effacé at dégagé height, tombé forward onto R (2nd) and pas de bourrée under turning 1/8 lt. to face DS, ending in fifth position demi-plié with L front (rt. to M5).

meas. &8:   Cts. &7&8: Two brisés over traveling sideways toward SR.

Medium Petit Allegro #1:

Advanced level

Music: March #2

Fifth position demi-plié croisé DSL (L5):

meas. &1:   Cts. &1&2: Failli turning 1/4 rt. to face DSR (M5), assemblé R over (L5-allongé 2nd-L5) turning 1/4 lt. to face DSL.

    Cts. &3&4: Failli turning 1/4 rt. to face DSR, grand battement R front (M5-H5) and grand fouetté en dehors with temps levé (1st arab.) turning 3/8 lt. to face SL.

meas. &2:   Cts. &5–6: Temps levé on L on upbeat, step R forward and grand battement L front (L5-M5-H5) into grand fouetté en dehors with temps levé (1st arab.) turning 1/2 rt. to face SR.

    Cts. &7&8: Straighten R while pivoting 3/8 lt. to face DSL with battement dégagé side, step L side, step R behind L (L5) and assemblé L under (allongé 2nd-L5).

meas. &3:   Cts. &1–4: Exact repeat of meas. 1.

meas. &4:   Cts. &5–6: Pivot 1/8 rt. to face DSL, step forward on R (L5-M5) and assemblé L over (L5-allongé 2nd-L5) while turning 1/4 rt. to face DSR.

Cts. &7–8: Two entrechat six, ending in fifth position demi-plié croisé, straighten supports.

Medium Petit Allegro #2:

Advanced level

Music: Schottische #3

Fifth position croisé DSR (L5):

meas. &1:   Cts. &1–2: Sissonne changée forward (M5-H5/2nd) turning 1/4 lt. to DSL, ending in attitude back croisé; step L forward (lt. to 2nd) and battement dégagé R front (L5); assemblé traveling forward, ending with R front (Cecchetti 3rd arab.).

Cts. &3–4: (M5-2nd/H5) on sissonne changée, repeat cts. &1–2 on other side to end facing DSR.

meas. &2:   Cts. &1–4: Exact repeat of meas. 1.

meas. &3:   Ct. &1: Sissonne passée back [L ends cou-de-pied back] (2nd/M5) turning 1/4 lt. to face DSL.

Ct. &2: Chassé lt. into second position (rt. to 2nd-allongé), release R side and assemblé with R front (L5) while traveling lt.

Cts. &3–4: (M5/2nd) on sissonne passée back [R ends cou-de-pied back], repeat cts. 1–2 of meas. 3 on other side to end facing DSR.

meas. &4:   Cts. &1–4: Exact repeat of meas. 3, ending DSR, straighten supports in fifth position croisé.

Grand Allegro #1:

> Advanced level
>
> Music: Big Waltz #3

Point tendu front croisé DSR (2nd):

meas. 8&a:	Step forward onto L, battement dégagé R front and glissade through fourth, landing on R.
meas. 1–2:	Complete glissade with L stepping through, assemblé R over (L5-allongé 2nd-L5) turning 1/4 lt. to face DSL.
meas. &3–4:	Failli turning 1/4 rt. to face DSR (M5), assemblé R over (L5-allongé 2nd-L5) turning 1/4 lt. to face DSL.
meas. &5:	Petit développé R forward (M5), piqué croisé 2nd arabesque (L5-croisé 2nd arab.).
meas. 6&a:	Fondu arabesque, two runs (2nd) turning 1/2 lt. to face USR.
meas. &7–8:	Step forward on L and tour jeté (L5-M5-H5-croisé 1st arab.), landing in croisé 1st arabesque facing DSL.
meas. &9:	Temps levé turning 3/4 lt. to face DSR with L gesture front croisé at dégagé height (M5), piqué arabesque onto L in croisé 2nd arabesque (L5-croisé 2nd arab.).
meas. 10&a:	Fondu arabesque, two runs (2nd) turning 1/2 rt. to face USL.
meas. &11–12:	Step forward on R and tour jeté (L5-M5-H5-croisé 1st arab.), landing in croisé 1st arabesque facing DSR.
meas. &13:	Temps levé turning 3/4 rt. to face DSL with R gesture front croisé at dégagé height (M5), run toward SL and exit (2nd-rt. to L5-lt. back diagonal/forward high arab.).

Grand Allegro #2:

Advanced level

Music: Grand Allegro 6/8

In this example, two counts are the equivalent of one measure of 6/8.

Point tendu front croisé DSR (2nd):

intro ct. 8:	Cts. 8&a: Step forward onto L (L5), battement dégagé R front and glissade through fourth, landing on R (M5).
meas. 1:	Cts. 1–2: Complete glissade with L stepping through, battement dégagé R front and cabriole front (H5/2nd), close R front in fifth position demi-plié effacé (M5).
meas. &a2:	Cts. &a3–4: Battement dégagé L back and glissade backward through fourth, landing on L and closing R front in fifth position demi-plié effacé; battement dégagé L back and cabriole back (L5-1st arab.), then tombé L through to front (M5).
meas. &a3–4:	Cts. &a5–8: Battement dégagé R front and glissade through fourth, landing on R with L stepping through; exact repeat of meas. 1–2.
meas. &a5–6&:	Cts. &a1–4&: Battement dégagé R front and glissade through fourth, landing on R with L stepping through; exact repeat of meas. 1–2, but temps levé on L with R petit développé front.
meas. 7:	Cts. 5&a6: Tombé forward on R (2nd) and pas de bourrée under, ending with L stepping forward.
meas. &8:	Cts. &7–8: Battement dégagé R front and glissade through fourth, landing on R with L stepping through (L5-M5); grand jeté développé (L5-Cecchetti 3rd arab.); tombé L through, ending in croisé long fourth (2nd).

INDEX TO COMBINATIONS' TECHNICAL DIFFICULTY

INDEX OF BALLET TERMINOLOGY

Since many steps occur with great frequency, not every example is listed here.